MW01419310

Not Enough of Her
Ordinary People Extraordinary Love

R.S. Duchin

AuthorHouse™
1663 Liberty Drive
Bloomington, IN 47403
www.authorhouse.com
Phone: 1-800-839-8640

© 2012 by R.S. Duchin. All rights reserved.

No part of this book may be reproduced, stored in a retrieval system, or transmitted by any means without the written permission of the author.

Published by AuthorHouse   10/29/2012

ISBN: 978-1-4685-5429-8 (sc)
ISBN: 978-1-4685-5428-1 (hc)
ISBN: 978-1-4685-5427-4 (e)

Library of Congress Control Number: 2012903127

Any people depicted in stock imagery provided by Thinkstock are models, and such images are being used for illustrative purposes only.
Certain stock imagery © Thinkstock.

This book is printed on acid-free paper.

Because of the dynamic nature of the Internet, any web addresses or links contained in this book may have changed since publication and may no longer be valid. The views expressed in this work are solely those of the author and do not necessarily reflect the views of the publisher, and the publisher hereby disclaims any responsibility for them.

Contents

Dedication		ix
Introduction		xi
Prologue		xvii
Chapter 1:	Susan's Family Origins	1
Chapter 2:	The Gellers	4
Chapter 3:	Steven	8
Chapter 4:	Robert	10
Chapter 5:	The Four Musketeers	14
Chapter 6:	Bob's Family Origins	16
Chapter 7:	Passive Aggressive	21
Chapter 8:	Spiritual Void	23
Chapter 9:	Rite of Passage	25
Chapter 10:	3rd Grade Trauma	29
Chapter 11:	Fun and . . . Nuclear Attacks?	31
Chapter 12:	B.T. and B.C.	35
Chapter 13:	Jr. High and High School	40
Chapter 14:	Summer Camp	45
Chapter 15:	Real World Lessons	51
	Ginger	53
	How Do Guys Survive? (Or: Dumb Things I Did and Lived to Tell About.)	54
	The Standoff	57
	Weapons of Less Destruction	60

Chapter 16:	Why Marry?	64
Chapter 17:	New Beginnings	67
Chapter 18:	Leaving Our Home Turf	71
Chapter 19:	Good Fortune Crumbles	76
Chapter 20:	Goodbye DASA	79
Chapter 21:	Escaping The Frying Pan	86
Chapter 22:	Off to California	88
Chapter 23:	Blunders and Blessings	90
Chapter 24:	Terrible Loneliness	94
Chapter 25:	The First 22 Days	97
Chapter 26:	Life Forever Changed	101
Chapter 27:	Triggers	103
Chapter 28:	The Great Fall, or, . . . The Great Performance?	105
Chapter 29:	Summer of 1957	108
Chapter 30:	First of 85 Love Letters	113
Chapter 31:	Everyone Saw Her Angel Wings	116
Chapter 32:	A Dark Season	118
Chapter 33:	Love Reborn	125
Chapter 34:	All My Love All My Love	130
Chapter 35:	Married At Last	132
Chapter 36:	Dreaded Reality: 100 Days	137
Chapter 37:	More Love Letters	145
Chapter 38:	Unexpected Intersection	153
Chapter 39:	My First Grief	156
Chapter 40:	Edward	170
Chapter 41:	New Friendships	180
Chapter 42:	Suralaya	189
Chapter 43:	Growing In Love	207
Chapter 44:	Time Drifting	209
Chapter 45:	Old Photographs	213

Chapter 46: A Terrible Secret Revealed..217
Chapter 47: Some Things Can't Be Changed..............................221
Chapter 48: Teen Dating In The 1950s..226
Chapter 49: Passion Recalled...231
Chapter 50: The Delight Of Love 233
Chapter 51: Passions Grow...240
Chapter 52: Is My Altered Life Worth Living?.............................243
Chapter 53: Letters To Grandchildren...274

Epilogue..289
Acknowledgments 293

Dedication

For my dear wife Susan, the light of my life, who taught me what real love is.

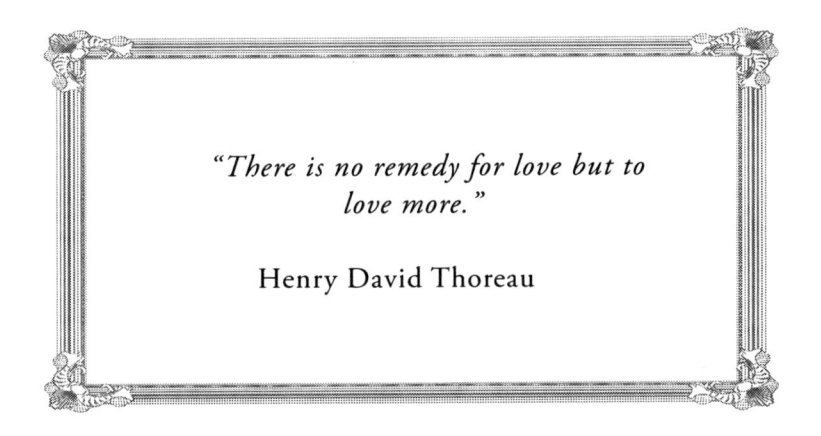

> *"There is no remedy for love but to love more."*
>
> Henry David Thoreau

And for my children, Eric, Andrea, and Adam, and my grandchildren: Jeffrey Gabriel Yepez (7 1/2), Joshua Andrew Yepez (5 1/2), Sadie Elise Duchin (6), Dillon Ellis Duchin (3 1/2), Logan Reed Duchin (1 1/2). I pray that this book will provide memories for my grandchildren that they would not otherwise have.

Introduction

I believe that at some level all of us are looking for something outside of ourselves that will explain life's difficult or mysterious issues.

We all believe in something that drives our actions, don't we? Even if we believe in nothing outside of ourself, that is the "something" we believe in. Whatever the case may be, our beliefs rule our behavior.

Are there "good" spirits and "bad" spirits in our world that influence our beliefs, and hence, our actions? In my experience there are indeed. However, I am not offering a theological diversion here. Each of us must confront our own demons and angels, real or imagined, on our own terms and in our own timing.

Yet one thing is inarguably true: nothing tests beliefs more than a crisis in our lives. In my case the worst crisis in my life came suddenly and overwhelmingly. Yet my belief system held fast. This has given me comfort and hope.

The pain of my great crisis was crushing and my future hopes and dreams became forever different from what I hoped or imagined they would be.

My spirit led me to want to write about life before, during, and after this upheaval. So I said to my spirit: Lead the way.

~ ~ ~ ~ ~ ~ ~ ~ ~ ~ ~

This story is about real flesh and blood people, real life events, and real love tested and refined in the furnaces of life. It is Susan and Bob Duchin's story.

Invariably, even something as precious, exciting, and fulfilling as true love creates wounds and scars along the way. Such is the complexity, frailty, and imperfection of our humanity.

However, I ask you this: Is there anything so especially satisfying and worthwhile as emerging victoriously after overcoming a trial? I think not. As a matter of fact, I know not.

So this isn't a fairy tale, although come to think of it, many so-called stories for children that contain love themes have their share of trials, tribulations, and tragedies. Consider: Cinderella, Snow White, Beauty and the Beast, Pinocchio, The Lion King, Finding Nemo, and on and on.

The Princess Bride, a cult classic, happens to be one of my all time favorite movies. Both my sons and I often have fun reciting and then responding to each other with memorized portions of the movie's clever and addictive script. The story is filled with heroes, a beautiful damsel in distress, villains, love, tragedy, adventure, duels, torture, monsters, nonsense, humor, and disappointment, before the "And they lived happily ever after" finally comes at the end of the story.

Real life love stories depart from stories like The Princess Bride in at least one very important respect. We know that in the classic fairy tales all will be well at the end. In real life, try as we might, we do not and cannot know the final outcome. Sometimes real life final outcomes are not very pretty.

I suppose that not knowing what's around the next bend in the road of life is one of the elements that adds excitement to the mix. Offering love to another person is a risky proposition. It puts us in a vulnerable place. We may ultimately find that offered love is rejected. There's risk in every action we take, isn't there? Just stepping outside our homes brings inherent risks of injury or death. No matter: We just can't know the outcomes of our own life stories until they happen.

This is a love story, and a story about love.

I believe that there are more than hairs to be split here. Love stories are typically associated with romance, which is not at all a bad thing. Susan and I had plenty of romance together. However, romance is not the engine of true love. Romance and its associated feelings especially in today's Western culture are often passed off as evidence of love. What a sad and treacherous myth this is!

Real love for another person, at its core, has little to do with emotional feelings. It has everything to do with conscious decisions to behave in certain ways for the benefit of the other person, not oneself. Real love, therefore, is intentionally, and willingly, sacrificial.

Romance is a welcome and delectable part of human interaction, but it's the icing on the cake, not the cake itself. The cake must be baked first. Baking, unlike cooking in general, is a more precise, very measured effort, not just a tossing together of ingredients as you go along; a pinch of this, a splash or dash of that, and perhaps some ingredients other than what the recipe calls for. Real love too, requires precision, and precision requires conscious, deliberate care and attention.

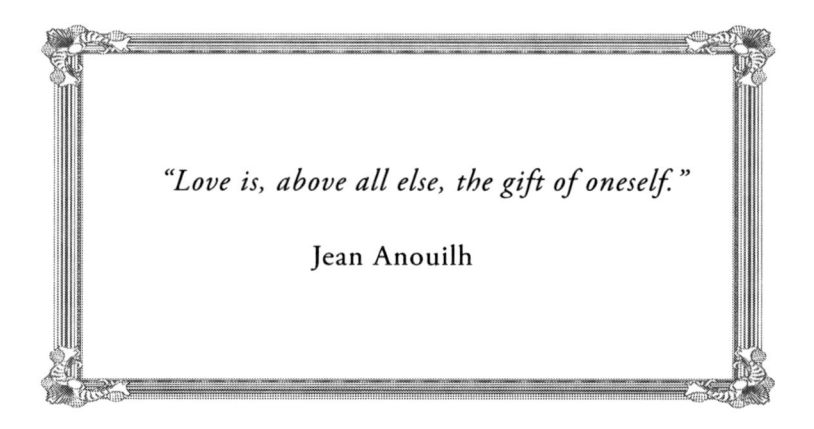

> "Love is, above all else, the gift of oneself."
>
> Jean Anouilh

Yet, a story about love, to be truly complete and satisfying to heart and mind, should include both love and romance. This story certainly does include both love and romance, and for having personally found this rare and precious completeness, I will be eternally grateful. What human condition could be more satisfying, more exciting, than to decide that you love someone, and then to also find romance with that special person?

I cannot imagine anything in the human experience that could come close to making a person feel that life is worth living, that life is bursting with completeness, than to be totally in love, and for that love to be returned just as totally.

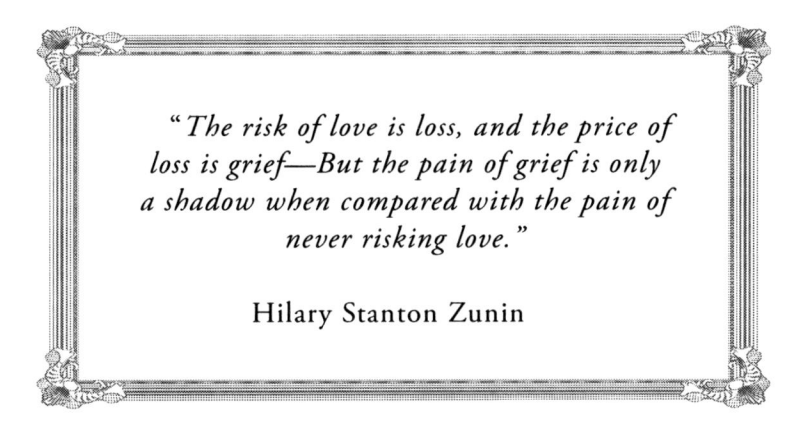

> *"The risk of love is loss, and the price of loss is grief—But the pain of grief is only a shadow when compared with the pain of never risking love."*
>
> Hilary Stanton Zunin

I hope that you will find something worthwhile for your own relationships as you read this collection of memories about love's transcendent and exquisite power in the lives of two ordinary people.

Prologue

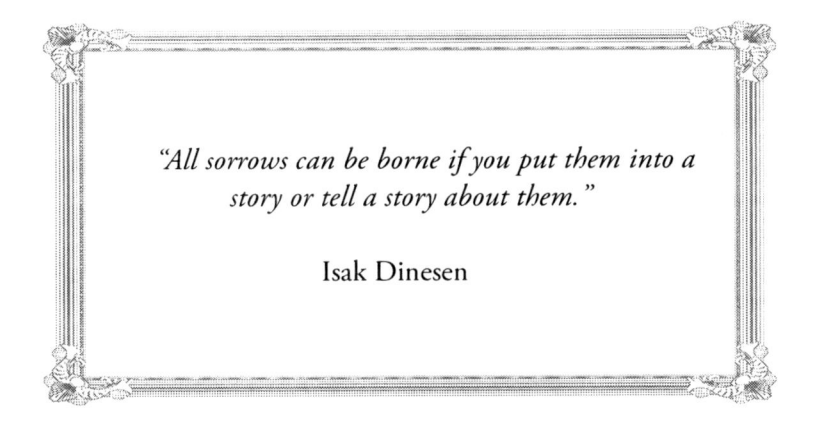

> *"All sorrows can be borne if you put them into a story or tell a story about them."*
>
> Isak Dinesen

Susan is so beautiful lying asleep next to me. Her body warmth is radiating across the scant inches of space between us. She had showered before retiring to bed, often a silent signal between us that making love was welcome. This long established part of our lives together was so deep-rooted that when I would hear the shower running in the evening, an early stage of physical arousal was involuntarily triggered. It was like a Pavlovian response; the sound of water caressing her body in the shower was all that was necessary to begin to create a sensual desire in me.

This night Susan went to bed before me, as she often did. We'd established an understanding between us that even if she was asleep when I eventually came to bed, if I wanted to make love, she would be a willing partner. This understanding was so like her: to not deny me the satisfaction of sexual pleasure even if I woke her from sound sleep in the middle of the night. Yet, I think that she liked this arrangement as much as I did. It added a spontaneity to our marriage that enhanced the excitement of anticipation.

I gently put my arm around her waist. Then I moved closer trying to not yet wake her. She had such a warm body temperature compared with mine. My arousal was steadily building while she lay still, our bodies now ever so lightly touching. I began to gently caress her and she then began to stir with a deeper than normal breath, telling me, without any words, that she was becoming awake. I moved my body to make firmer contact with hers, our bodies slowly and gently molding together.

She moaned softly with pleasure in her tone, another signal encouraging me to continue my approach. I pressed more tightly against her. She then rolled toward me seeking my kisses. Susan's lips were so soft and warm, the taste of her so sweet, and in moments our mouths were melted together.

Kissing further heated our passions. We touched each other with loving pleasure. Passion continued to climb, inevitably, naturally. I was lost in ever heightening waves of pleasure and I wanted to return to her as much pleasure as I could possibly give. We traded delights.

This was ecstasy beyond words. A marvelous part of our marriage, pleasuring each other without shame, hesitation, or selfishness.

Through all our years of marriage our faithfulness to each other made our intimacy extraordinarily special.

When our passion was finally spent we relaxed in each other's arms covered with a gloss of perspiration, gradually allowing our pounding heartbeats and breathlessness to normalize. We then whispered a few loving words to each other, kissed once more, and went to sleep.

But something wasn't quite right. Though this was a typical scenario when we made love, instead of now going to sleep for the rest of the night, I awoke.

I looked toward Susan's side of our bed and it was empty. Then it suddenly hit me. This had been a dream! It wasn't real. It was a desire fulfilled only in the almost-reality of my mind.

You see, my sweet Susan, the love of my life, my darling wife, the other half of my very being, and my only lover for 47 years, was gone. Susan had died with stunning suddenness six months earlier.

I miss her so much that I sometimes feel that I want to die to be with her again. This dream seemed so real, and for this I am thankful. But, oh, how I miss my sweet Susan!

If ever two souls were designed to be intimately mated, they were ours. The absence of her love, not just the physical love, is like having half of my very being ripped away.

Perhaps I'll survive but I'll never heal from this terrible wound, this terrible loss. I will never stop loving her or dreaming about her.

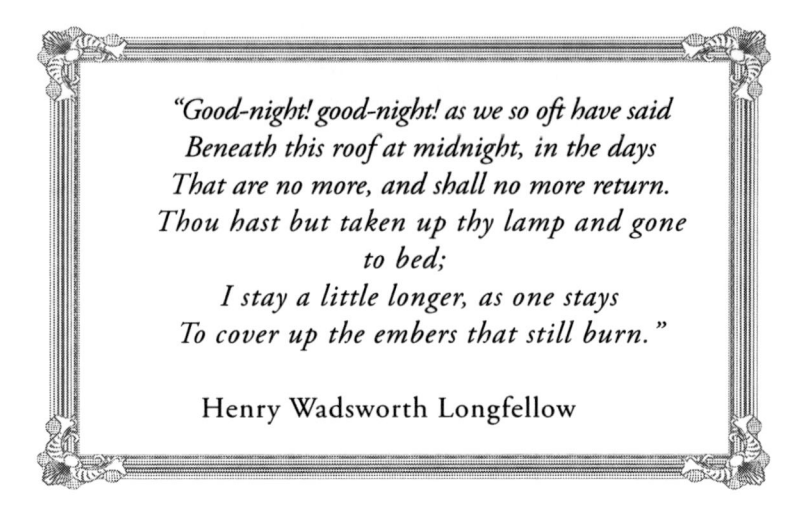

> "Good-night! good-night! as we so oft have said
> Beneath this roof at midnight, in the days
> That are no more, and shall no more return.
> Thou hast but taken up thy lamp and gone to bed;
> I stay a little longer, as one stays
> To cover up the embers that still burn."
>
> Henry Wadsworth Longfellow

My writings began to take shape in the months following Susan's sudden death when my emotions and recollections of our lives together for 47 years were most heightened. Writing about us helped me to fill an aching hole in my heart that cloaked my day-to-day existence. I intended to share what I was writing with my children as a written memorial of their parents' lives together. Then they could share it with their children—our five grandchildren—most of whom will not remember their loving grandmother Susan, because sadly, they were too young when she died.

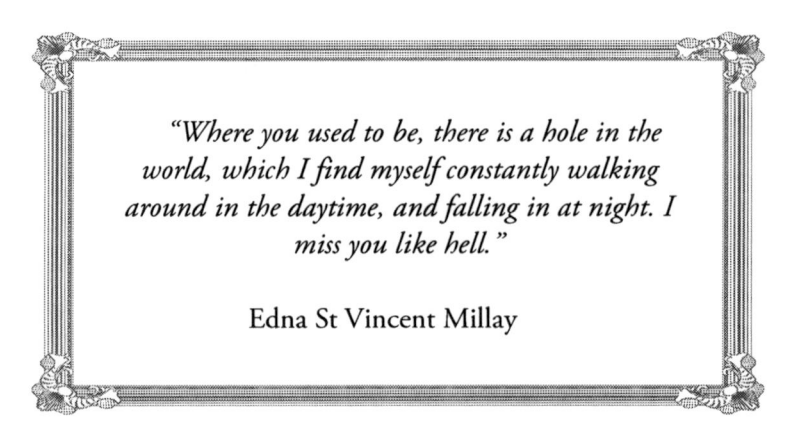

> "Where you used to be, there is a hole in the world, which I find myself constantly walking around in the daytime, and falling in at night. I miss you like hell."
>
> Edna St Vincent Millay

Susan 2006

Chapter 1

Susan's Family Origins

Susan at 14, when I first met her, was a lovely and vibrant young girl. Five feet three inches tall, very fair-skinned and clear complexioned, a few scattered freckles across her nose, blonde hair, big, bright, blue eyes, and other facial features that belied her Eastern European ancestry.

Her grandparents had emigrated from Poland. The paternal side of her family settled for a time in Israel, where her father was born, thus making him a Sabra, a native-born Israeli. The maternal side of her family lived in England before they eventually came and settled in the United States.

Looking at her parents, her older brother Robert, and her grandparents on both sides of her family, you would see undeniable Eastern European features: stocky people of average to below average height, and their noses would be a strong clue. While not rendering their faces unattractive on the whole, their noses were prominent features, as is not unusual for people from Eastern Europe, especially Jewish people. After all, the Jewish people are descended from the

Hebrew people of the ancient Middle East. Abraham, the Abraham of the Old Testament, came from the city of Ur. On today's modern map of the Middle East the city of Ur would be in Iraq. Ironic, isn't it? The patriarch of the Hebrew people was an Iraqi!

By the way, I'm not concerned about being accused of racial profiling, a hot button in our culture today. My lack of concern is due to the fact that I am also of Jewish Eastern European ancestry, and proud of it. So, I give myself a free pass on this issue.

Consider the typical facial features of Middle Eastern peoples. Jewish or non-Jewish, these Semitic peoples have facial characteristics that many Americans have come to associate with 'looking Jewish'. That is a ridiculous thought process. How does a person look like a religion? Can you walk down the street and pick out a Catholic? A Methodist? A Mormon? . . . based on physical characteristics? Of course you can't.

When you give it even cursory thought, 'looking Jewish' simply means looking Eastern European, where the majority of the modern world's Jews lived until, in particular, the horrendous persecutions of Jews in the eighteenth and nineteenth centuries in that part of the world.

Americans live in a country with Jewish people who have been well-assimilated into our culture, especially on the East coast where there are large clusters of people of Jewish ancestry. We Americans much less frequently rub elbows with other Semitic peoples, who also 'look Jewish'.

This facial landmarking of prominent physical Jewish features was less true for Susan and her younger brother, Steven. Susan and

Steven simply came out of the mold with clear differences from the majority of their family members. Their features were more, let's say, balanced. It doesn't take much to change a person's overall appearance. Just enlarge or diminish a nose a bit, give them bigger or smaller ears or lips, make the eyes a different shape or size or color, change hair texture, hair color or skin tone. Any of these alterations even singly could make the person look like someone very different. Maybe the good Lord just bestowed on the only female child of the Geller family, all the separate, delightful, facial features that artfully blended would cause most observers to think: "That's a very pretty girl!" (And she doesn't 'look Jewish'.)

Chapter 2

The Gellers

I spent many days with Susan at her parents' apartment in the Bronx, New York, and at family gatherings at the homes of her grandparents, aunts and uncles. These were often pleasant times mostly because I was with Susan. Her family was a lot different from mine. I'm not making a qualitative judgment here, just an observation after years of close contact with them. You might say that many of Susan's clan were eccentric. Here are a few examples.

Susan's older brother Robert, and younger brother Steven, her mother and father, and her mother's brother Jerry, were amateur musicians. As you might expect, there was almost always something musical happening when they were together.

Susan's mother, Rose, had a beautiful singing voice and often sang at family gatherings. It was the only exceptional thing that I can think of to say about her. I would have much preferred that she were an exceptional mother instead, or at least a good cook. Sadly, she did not provide her daughter the protection and tenderness that Susan needed.

Her cooking was mediocre at best. Meals were unimaginative, recipes were bland, meat was usually overcooked. Mealtimes which I often shared with them were not highlights of my life. Oh the things we tolerate for love!

Susan's father, Louis, and both her brothers, were self-taught on the piano and often played and wrote songs purely for family consumption, though Steven thought he had a shot at recording and publishing a very catchy rock & roll tune that he wrote. I actually liked it and heard it many times over the years. But it went nowhere. Rose's brother Jerry played piano and favored show tunes, with Rose often singing when he played. Susan loved to sing but definitely did not inherit her mother's singing giftedness. She didn't care; she just loved to sing. I often teased her about it but I enjoyed watching her enjoy herself.

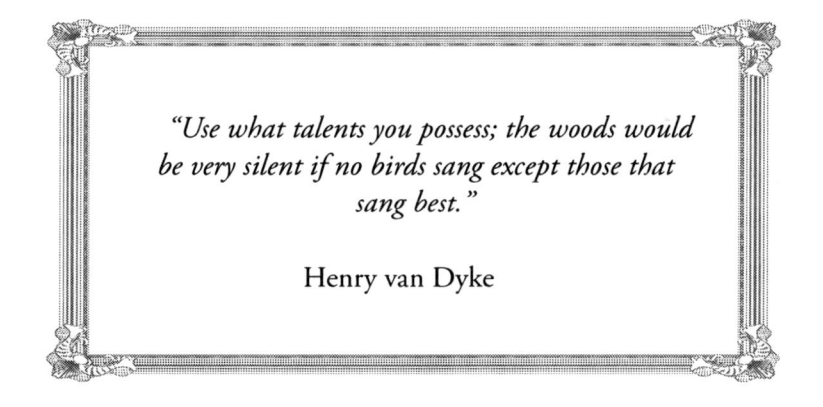

> *"Use what talents you possess; the woods would be very silent if no birds sang except those that sang best."*
>
> Henry van Dyke

So it might be accurate to state that the Geller family were a group of frustrated musical show-people. There was also an uncle of Susan's, on her mother's side, named Harry. He was British, and made his living as an auctioneer, another kind of stage performer. The Gellers had fun together and I enjoyed being part of their lively get-togethers often punctuated with music.

Even their dog, "Rusty", was eccentric, and whacky. Rusty was Louis' sidekick. They would often 'perform' together, Louis roller skating in their apartment. Yup, that's what I said, rollerskating in the house with Rusty chasing and barking like crazy, or doing other typical dog tricks at Louis' commands. I told you they were eccentric. Not infrequently Rusty would chomp onto my pants cuffs for no sane reason, then growl and pull. Fun game for Rusty, a pain in the butt for me. I liked dogs and had my own dog, a Cocker Spaniel named "Ginger", but I could have lived a very contented life if Rusty had never existed. P.S. Rusty was struck and killed by a car while Steven was walking him one day. And, no, I was not the driver. That's my story and I'm sticking to it.

Louis Geller's parents, sisters, and many other relatives also lived in the Bronx. So I got to know Susan's family well. They were nice to me and treated me like one of the family.

Susan's grandfather Sam, on her mother's side, owned a women's hat store in New Jersey, and lived with his wife, Hilda, in a small apartment in the back of the store. Susan loved to visit there and try on hats. I fondly referred to him (not to his face) as grandpa Buddha, because of his short stature and big belly. I enjoyed the British accents of this side of Susan's family and learned many British colloquialisms, especially off-color expressions, which I got a real kick out of. One of Susan's aunts often called me a "soppy bugger", which loosely translated means a "silly chap". It could also mean a "contemptible chap", which I choose to believe she did not mean.

Her maternal grandfather, Hillel, owned a handbag manufacturing company in the Bronx. Susan's father worked for his father in this business. No surprise that Susan always had many handbags and they were free! A gal's dream come true, isn't it? Grandpa Hillel was a very observant Jew, spending a great deal of time in his synagogue. He was Orthodox to the extreme. Here's just one example. Because the Bible states that no work is to be done on the Sabbath, on Friday night, the traditional beginning of the Jewish Sabbath, grandpa Hillel would turn all the lights on in the house. Why? Because flipping a light switch was "work".

I found out from Susan at a point in our relationship before we were engaged to be married, that her mother didn't want her to marry me. There was no specific reason ever given, and I never found out why, or, I just can't remember getting any explanation from Susan. I really didn't care much because it was not her mother that had a hold on Susan, it was her father. He didn't harbor the same feeling about me, at least as I perceived things.

Chapter 3

Steven

When Susan's younger brother Steven was 17, he was caught and arrested along with some friends for attempting to steal a car. It was probably just for a joy ride but nonetheless a serious crime. When he went to court the judge gave him two choices: accept a conviction and go to jail, or join the military. Steven chose the military and joined the U.S. Marine Corps for a two year hitch, a good part of which he served on the South Pacific island of Okinawa. Not surprisingly he returned more mature, more disciplined, and with an honorable discharge. Steven liked to act and look tough but he had a soft heart.

Steven joined his mother's brother Michael's business which was, at first, repairing sewing machines. Later the business morphed into designing and installing automated conveyor systems. Some of their contracts were for large and complex projects and involved Steven's traveling to distant job sites for weeks at a time to supervise construction. He and Michael did this successfully for many years.

Now, sadly, Steven is a very sick man, having contracted a rare disease and been unable to work for years. He's been blessed to have his military veteran's medical benefits.

When he was a teenager, Steven, like his older brother, got a girl pregnant and then married her. They eventually had two sons and a daughter before they divorced, and now he has a bunch of grandkids and great-grandkids who all live near his home. He remarried and did not have any children with his second wife. He became, and still is, active in his local synagogue. Who woulda thunk; Steven active in a church!

Steven and Susan had an estranged relationship for a few years after their mother Rose died until about six months before Susan died, when Steven broke his silence and called his sister. Susan was so happy to connect again with her brother, whom she loved, the only living member of her immediate family.

I've been keeping in touch with Steven since Susan died and we're exchanging old photos. He has sent me pictures of Susan between the ages of two and twelve which are so precious to me. I have some pictures of Susan at various ages, but only one of her as a little girl. So I'm filling in blanks as I build a picture history of her life. She was so adorable as a child and every time I look at these pictures I can't help but smile. This is very good therapy for my aching heart.

Chapter 4

Robert

Susan's older brother Robert had a group of pals who regularly stopped in at the Geller household to hang with Robert. I vaguely remember them as a colorful bunch. They all had funny nicknames like "Gimpy," sort of like comic book characters. Robert was a year or so older than me.

Robert went on to become a pretty decent professional jazz pianist using the stage name of Bob Gale, and he held many jobs unrelated to music while performing music gigs here and there in the evenings and on weekends. One of the jobs he had for quite a few years was with a notable Oriental rug dealer in Manhattan. Robert learned the business quickly: the intricacies of identifying specific styles of rugs, the geographic regions they were woven in, and most importantly to him, the dollar values.

The designation "Oriental rug" has a broad context which includes rugs from China, but which more typically refers to rugs hand-made in Persia (now Iran), hence, "Persian rugs", and hand-made rugs from the Balkans, generally referred to as "Caucasian rugs" because of the prominence of the Caucasus Mountains in that part of the world.

When Susan and I moved from New York City to North Andover, Massachusetts, in the late 1960s, her brother Robert, who had become a freelance rug dealer, would make a swing through the New England area a few times a year literally going door to door looking for rugs to buy and then resell. He got me very interested in Oriental rugs. I saw them as unique, beautiful, handmade works of art. Robert saw them as a means to make money.

In those days there were many people who had old Persian rugs in their homes, perhaps inherited from a relative, often stored away in an attic or basement. After all, New England is the oldest region of the country. The town we lived in had been established in the 1600s. So, antiques were in great abundance. Robert found many rare and valuable rugs in this way and was able to turn them over for, in some cases, thousands of dollars, having paid hundreds or less.

When he visited and stayed with us, I sometimes went along with him on his local rug hunts just to hang out together. I'd acquired a good working knowledge of rugs and at least could tell when I spotted something valuable and whether the ticket price was reasonable or not. There was an antique shop in Lawrence, Massachusetts, a city just a few miles northeast from where we were living. The shop was called the "Second Hand Store," and it always had some Oriental rugs for sale. I'd gotten to know Harold Landy, the owner, because Susan and I had bought a number of furniture items for our home from him. He had a young assistant who was French and had one blind eye. He was an arrogant jerk. Frenchie (whose real name I don't remember) and Robert did not get along, and sometimes Robert would ask me to negotiate for a rug that he knew Frenchie would give him a hard time about, or might just not sell it to him at all just to prove that he had the power to do so.

One time, when Robert and I were out together rug hunting, I found a nice "Sarouk", a relatively common and very identifiable style and design of Persian rug. It was about 4'x6' in size, hanging across a rope line strung in the back of this incredibly cluttered store. I loved this place because it was like searching for treasure in a jungle of junk.

Harold wasn't there that day so Frenchie was in charge. I knew, as did Robert, that the owner was knowledgeable about rugs but Frenchie . . . not so much. Robert hadn't yet seen the Sarouk that I had found and the price that Frenchie quoted me was low. I knew then and there that I wanted this rug for my home. So I proceeded to take advantage of the opportunity, and milking my rapport with Frenchie, I negotiated a ridiculously low price. I bought the rug.

When I showed it to Robert and told him that I'd bought it, he got angry, telling me that he was trying to make a living buying and selling rugs and that I was stealing this one out from under him. Puhleez! What an actor. I could almost hear the violins in the background. At most he might make fifty dollars profit on this rug, and, besides, he had a van load of rugs sitting out by the curb, including some particularly valuable finds that would bring him thousands in profit. It was a nice haul for him and he was being melodramatic over this one decent, but very average rug that I had just happened to spot first and buy for myself. We had no prior agreement that I couldn't buy a rug while I was with him, an agreement I probably wouldn't have made anyway.

He carried on about this for hours and from time to time in years to come, it came up, but more as a lighthearted remembrance of this one time that I scored on a rug that he missed. I still have the rug and it's a wonderful reminder of this fun adventure with my friend and brother-in-law.

Robert led an unhealthy lifestyle and, sadly, died of a heart attack in his early sixties. His last job was playing piano in the lounge on a cruise ship. Robert and I got along well. I'm sure it helped that we both loved jazz. When Robert got married, he and his wife Deborah, and Susan and I, became close friends often getting together as couples to hang out and play cards. It was always the guys against the gals in our card games and Robert and I developed not too subtle signals to cheat the girls, who would then get dramatically indignant when they caught us. It was just part of our fun together. Robert and Deborah had one child, a daughter, Michele, who was adorable as a child and grew to be a lovely, sweet woman. Michele's disposition was much like her mother's, and her aunt Susan's.

I always fantasized about being a jazz drummer and got a professional set of drums when I was in my 30s when Susan and I were living in Massachusetts with our first child, Eric. I loved to play along with recorded jazz music as a way to let off steam. When her brother Robert came to visit us he'd bring a portable keyboard and we would jam together. Robert was also our supplier of marijuana, which I think notably improved my playing. Perception is reality.

Chapter 5

The Four Musketeers

When Susan and I began seeing a lot of each other I got to know her closest friends very well. There were three girlfriends that Susan was especially close with: "little big Susan" (no, not a Native American name), Andrea, and Muriel. Little big Susan lived in the same apartment building as my Susan.

Here's the story about the name. The other Susan was referred to as "little big Susan" because she was shorter and had large breasts. My Susan was referred to as "big little Susan" . . . you get the picture. I always thought this was cute and funny. By the way, my Susan's breasts were by no means small, they just weren't large. As much as a lot of guys rave about big boobs, this never was much of an issue for me. To me, a pretty face was where attraction started. Followed by nice legs and a curvy torso. The boob thing was at the bottom of my list. Still is. You know what some guys say about boobs: More than a handful is wasted.

I remember her friends coming over to Susan's apartment and yakking and dancing to rock & roll music. Susan loved to dance. I was very content watching her swing and bounce with her girlfriends as they practiced doing the Lindy. I could never get the hang of it, and frankly, found it erotic for girls to shake, bounce and spin, accentuating the beauty of the female form that God created. It intimidated and aroused me at the same time. But I sure liked to watch.

Andrea and Muriel lived just a block away but we never spent much time in their families' apartments. Most of the time they congregated in the Geller's apartment, or in the nicer weather just hung out in the streets nearby. Andrea was a very pretty, vivacious girl, with a winning smile and a mischievous sparkle in her eyes. Little big Susan was cute and curvy, had a gentle demeanor, but wasn't as pretty as Susan and Andrea. Muriel had lovely dark hair, but a crooked nose dominated her otherwise pleasant facial features.

These "four musketeers" went to dances together at the local community center and loved to go roller skating at a roller rink just a short bus ride away. I was invited at times but it just wasn't my thing.

Oddly, I have no recollection of any of the other three girls having boyfriends during the time that I was dating Susan.

Chapter 6

Bob's Family Origins

I think of my past more frequently now that there are fewer future years to look forward to than the number of past years that I've lived. As my memory begins to dim as part of the normal aging process, I believe that it is sensible to transmit memories into written form while I can. Why bother? Because it will be a gift to my children and their offspring to help them to better understand their roots. This is something that I wish that my parents had done.

I came to be interested in my family's history late in the game because so many relatives and friends of the family with important and precious memories were already gone or too old to remember details that would enrich a tapestry of life. I have very fond memories of my grandparents and other close relatives but lots of details are now unfortunately beyond capture.

Of course I know myself and my family better than I know Susan and her family. So, there is more story to tell here than there is for her.

My ancestry is Russian Jewish. My grandparents fled religious persecution even though my paternal grandfather served in the Russian military. This is a fact that has always irked me; that his country would accept his military service, and then persecute him for his religious heritage. One of my most precious possessions is an oval-framed, colorized photo-portrait of my grandfather, Abraham Duchin, in his Russian army uniform, with his handlebar mustache. I also have a photo of him showing all of his uniform including shiny high cavalry boots. He was a very dashing young soldier.

Though my maternal grandfather, Harry, and my paternal grandmother, Lena, looked classically Eastern European, their counterparts did not. Grandpa Abraham (paternal), and grandma Sarah (maternal), had more balanced and finer facial features, and my parents, Dick and Fay Duchin, didn't 'look Jewish' either, in the way that I described earlier.

My dad's occupation was selling medical supplies and equipment to hospitals and other healthcare providers primarily in the greater New York City metropolitan area. One of his biggest business accounts had a group of facilities spread around the city administered by a Catholic order of nuns called Little Sisters of the Poor. I remember on several occasions my father expressing concern that he might lose this important part of his livelihood if they discovered that he was Jewish. This was not an unreasonable fear because he'd already lost business from another Catholic organization for this very reason. Dad didn't hide the fact that he was Jewish. But he did not volunteer it either. Business was business.

I remember that dad would buy a new car every two years because of the high mileage that he logged, and the cars were always black with black-walled tires. This was his way of appearing modest to the nuns that he did so much business with. From 1951 on, dad bought a new Buick every two years until he was retired, keeping his last Buick, a 1990 model, until he was well into his 80s, and no longer fit to drive safely. The Buicks of the 1950s and 1960s were built more solidly than todays Humvees, and might better survive combat missions. Dad did not buy cars with power steering or air conditioning until the 1970s. I think that this was for purely financial reasons.

Dad taught me to drive in his 1957 Buick "Special", two tons of no nonsense steel, 300 horsepower under the hood, with no power steering! Here's how the driving lessons went. Early on weekend mornings, and I mean early, while even the birds were still snoring, he would drive me from the Bronx to quiet suburban streets in Yonkers, New York, just outside the New York City limits. Sleepy suburbia; no other cars moving about. We lived in the northeastern part of the Bronx, so Yonkers was just 10 minutes north. When I progressed in my driving skills dad would let me drive from the Bronx to Yonkers on the Bronx River Parkway. If he felt that I was driving too fast he had the habit of tapping his foot loudly on the passenger side floorboard signaling me that my foot was too heavy on the gas pedal. It was a very effective nonverbal signal. It was also very annoying.

Dad would park the car on a residential street and then exchange places with me. He told me to just keep driving slowly around the same block and every time I saw a parking spot that looked like it would fit the monster Buick, I was to parallel park the car. You see, in New York City, parking spaces were often very hard to find and all of them required parallel parking, the trickiest part of driving a car, far easier, of course, with power steering. Dad was determined to ensure that I could masterfully parallel park the Buick (did I say without power steering?).

Have you ever tried to parallel park a 1957 Buick without power steering or air conditioning? Anyone can parallel park a car—eventually. It might take a few attempts, a few forward and reverse maneuvers, maybe even a few light taps against the cars parked in front or behind. I've witnessed New York drivers squeeze into tight parking spots and intentionally use their vehicles to push the car in front or behind to make room for their car. God forbid that I should even slightly kiss another vehicle with dad in the car! New York drivers are not the most patient folks on the planet. So, holding up traffic because some fool was screwing up an attempt to parallel park was more than justification for leaning long and hard on their car horns and yelling words of . . . well let's just say that they were motivating terms but not encouraging terms.

When my dad, the parking Nazi, was finally satisfied with my prowess he allowed me to take my driving test at age 17, which I passed with flying colors.

Here's an especially vivid memory that made a distinct stamp on my life. I was about 14 years old and my brother Edward, was 9. My dad came home from work one day and was very excited. He told us that when he called on the Little Sisters of the Poor that day, the Mother Superior, who essentially was the CEO of the Catholic Order, and who made all the purchasing decisions, greeted him, and seemingly out of the blue, asked him if he was Jewish. This stunned him, and he told us that he braced himself to lose his most important business account because he had decided that he would not lie about being Jewish. With deeply mixed emotions he looked the Mother Superior in the eye and answered, "Yes, I'm Jewish", and then waited for darkly hooded men to leap from the shadows and drag him away to be tortured and burned at the stake.

As dad continued the story, much to his amazement, the Mother Superior looked at him, smiled warmly, and said: "Do you know that our Lord Jesus Christ was a Jew?" As if this unexpected statement wasn't enough of a shock, she escorted him on a grand tour of the facility, and his business relationship was more deeply cemented. My family was truly thrilled by this story, and it was good reason to rejoice for this very middle-class family, living in a two bedroom, one bath, rent-controlled, Bronx, New York, tenement apartment.

Chapter 7

Passive Aggressive

I believe that my parents would agree that I was a well-behaved child. Yet I had a passive-aggressive streak running through my psyche that, of course, I couldn't understand when I was a kid, but which later in life I came to recognize and tried to deal with through professional therapy.

So, here I am, from age seven to around 11 or 12, very obedient to mom and dad—let's say 90% of the time—who created havoc on the street where we lived by picking fights and beating up most boys my age who just happened to cross my path. Of course it always feels good to be the winner of a fight, but not to be the parents of a fighter. For some few years there was a steady stream of parents knocking on our apartment door or calling on the phone to complain to my mother (dad was conveniently at work during the day) that "your Bobby just beat up my . . . (fill in the blank)".

Mom of course would apologize, promise to deal with me, and would then have a heart-to-heart with me, or if the offense seemed more severe than normal, I'd get the "just wait till your father gets home!" routine. That threat never put the fear of God, or the fear of anything for that matter into me, because my father never laid a hand on me. Never. It was mom whom I dreaded. Not in the sense that she would do me irreparable physical damage, but because she was the disciplinarian in the family, and she wouldn't hesitate to spank me, wash out my mouth with soap if I uttered a bad word, or when I got older and bigger physically, so that her spankings didn't amount to much other than my mild amusement, she might just use a belt, or whack me with a shoe. These days parents get arrested for stuff like this.

Sound like a horrible mother? NO WAY! I adored my mother. I adored her for taking responsibility for teaching me right from wrong, assuring that I understood that there were boundaries to behavior, and that if boundaries were crossed there was a price to pay for the transgression. In so many words, even at this young age, she was teaching me how to be a good person and a good parent. My dad wasn't a bad parent. He was just soft when it came to child discipline.

Chapter 8

Spiritual Void

My parents weren't religious people in the sense that they expressed a belief in God, prayed, read the Bible, attended a synagogue, or articulated to me the value of any of these things. Yet we celebrated certain holy times on the Jewish calendar intentionally, but hollowly. Like all of our friends and neighbors.

We lit candles for Hannukah, commemorating the miracle of the single day supply of oil found in the desecrated temple in Jerusalem, which then burned for eight days.

We got together with other family members for Passover Seders, sometimes reading aloud from the Haggadah to commemorate the ancient Hebrews' miraculous rescue from slavery in Egypt. We casually observed the Jewish New Year, Rosh Hashanah.

Yom Kippur is the annual day of atonement for Jews, the holiest of the Jewish holy days. Fasting on Yom Kippur is a symbolic gesture of penance for the forgiveness of sins. Thereafter you could begin a new year racking up sins to your heart's content and then unload them again the following Yom Kippur. Such a deal! My mother would fast on Yom Kippur. When I was older I joined her in fasting. My dad did not fast. The best thing of all was that in New York City, with a population that was around 25% Jewish at that time of my life, the public schools closed on the Jewish holidays. There really is a God!

My mom did something spiritual that was very, very special to me. I'm sure that she was following what she learned from her mother, my beloved grandma Sarah. Every Friday night at sundown, the start of the traditional Jewish Sabbath, my mother would put a shawl over her head, light two candles, and say a prayer over the candles while slowly moving her outraised hands above the candle flames as though she was waving the light of the candles Heavenward. I have no recollection of what she prayed, yet this brief, weekly act of spiritual predictability was something that I loved to watch her do. It fascinated and mystified me, and it touched something deep within my heart.

So, we were secular Jews. A hard working dad, a dedicated stay-at-home mom, living a modest middle-class existence in the heart of the Bronx, New York, surrounded by other secular Jewish families. However, even secular Jewish boys did not get to escape the important ritual known as "Bar Mitzvah," which literally means, "son of commandment". This occurred at the age of 13. It symbolized a male reaching the age of maturity in the Jewish faith, now responsible for his own actions. Though it was typically celebrated by having a big party with relatives and friends, and the expectation of a pile of gifts, usually cash, it was getting to the party part that was the catch; the training for the Bar Mitzvah ceremony, and the accompanying synagogue ritual.

Chapter 9

Rite of Passage

Starting a year or so before the date of my Bar Mitzvah, I was enrolled in a Hebrew school that was run by the rabbi of a local Orthodox synagogue where the school was housed. I was required to attend Hebrew school at the synagogue for an hour or so every day after I finished my day in public school. Rabbi Israel J. Harris was the teacher, and he was a stern taskmaster. Originally from South Africa, Rabbi Harris spoke in heavily accented English and had some colorful expressions that he would use at certain times. For example, when he wanted to strongly emphasize something, he would first say: "I vont you to know".

More often than I'd like to admit, Rabbi Harris would become annoyed with me because I was messing around and disrupting the class. He would say to me, heavily rolling the R's of my name in a gutteral tone, and shaking his finger menacingly in my direction: "RRRRRobert, I'm going to smeck your face!" I don't remember him ever actually 'smecking' my face, or anyone else's for that matter, but we all found it to be a very funny expression, and I laugh about it to this day with old friends who were in my Hebrew class.

The curriculum was intended to prepare each student to be able to successfully read aloud, directly from the synagogue Torah scroll, in front of the entire congregation, a predetermined section of the Bible. Not only read it, but chant it!

In synagogue Sabbath services on Saturday mornings the same Bible verses from the Law (the first five books of the Old Testament), and from the Prophets, are read on the same day every year in accordance with the Jewish calendar. Thus it is simple to know in advance, for any Saturday service, which verses from the Bible would be read. When the date of a boy's Bar Mitzvah was set, so was the "Haftorah"—those Bible verses that would be read by the Bar Mitzvah boy during that particular Saturday service.

This was a very daunting prospect for 12 year old kids, none of whom could read a word of Hebrew at the outset. Not only was this scary enough, the synagogue Torah scroll was covered with an elaborately embroidered velvet sleeve, stood about three feet tall, and was kept in a veiled compartment in the wall of the synagogue. The Torah scroll was hand written, the paper of which was considered too holy to touch with a bare hand, contained no vowels, which in other more common Hebrew documents, such as our Hebrew school textbooks, were included to show how to correctly pronounce letters and words.

Thus began the task of learning to read Hebrew, an ancient language, its letters utterly different from the English alphabet. If that was not difficult enough, Hebrew is read from right to left. Oy Vey! This was quite a challenge, but it was a rite of passage and an old tradition that every Jewish parent's sons endured, and so a small group of us slogged through it together for a year.

Besides learning to read Hebrew, which we eventually were able to do, later in our schooling we were taught other ancient rituals that observant Jewish men regularly performed. No, get the picture of animal sacrifices and secret handshakes out of your head. These were very tame and very arcane things such as wearing a black leather headband containing a small leather box that was strapped to the middle of the forehead, inside of which was specific Scripture, and wrapping "Tefillin," a black leather strap, around the forearm with a precise number of turns, and only in one specified direction. I dutifully learned these things which were very odd to me and which did not strike any spiritual chords whatsoever. Finally I was shown the Haftorah that I would be required to read on the fateful day of my Bar Mitzvah, and taught the chant that was part of the ceremony.

The big day inevitably came and I was scared out of my wits. Not so much because my family was present, or that I wasn't prepared, but because I was to perform in front of the rabbi and the elders of the synagogue who occupied the front rows. I wondered if they would stone me to death if I screwed up.

Yet all went as planned and I never stepped foot in a synagogue again with the intention of worshipping. Why not? Because, sadly, everything we learned was by rote. I could now read Hebrew fluently but I could not translate into English more than a few words of what I was reading, nor was I aware of the portion of the Bible the words came from. How sad. What a waste.

Because of the extent of repetition during Hebrew school training, the first lines of my Haftorah were branded into my mind and I remember them even to this day. It wasn't until 32 years later, after I'd become a practicing Christian, that I became curious enough to try to find out what the words meant that I blindly recited on the day of my Bar Mitzvah, and from what part of the Bible they were from. The part that I remember so clearly are beautiful Old Testament words from the book of the Prophet Isaiah, who wrote them around 700 B.C. The words, translated from the Hebrew, are: *"Arise, shine, for your light has come and the glory of the Lord has risen upon you."*

Having been a Christian for 10 years when I discovered the translation of my Bar Mitzvah Haftorah, chills ran up my spine as it struck me that so many years before, when I had no idea what the words I was learning meant in English, and having little interest in finding out, God was blessing me with a prophetic word about my future connection with Him. I consider this a true miracle. To me a miracle is something that has no natural explanation. Coincidence? Coincidence doesn't cut it for me. Everything happens for a reason.

Chapter 10

3rd Grade Trauma

Because I've seen so many photos from my childhood, and still remember many stories told to me about when I was a little rascal, it's sometimes difficult to distinguish what is my own firsthand memory from something that was implanted into my mind by others.

I believe that one of my earliest firsthand memories is from the third grade, age eight. I remember my third grade teacher's name, and I can vividly picture her face. Miss Kaminetsky. Blonde hair, nice looking, thick-rimmed glasses . . . but in 1948, weren't all eyeglasses thick-rimmed? I had been proudly elected or selected president of the class. I have no idea what I did to deserve this honor. Was it a premonition of future greatness? Had my teacher and classmates seen some innate special quality in me that was to continue to blossom as time went on? I haven't got a clue!

As the fates would have it the president was soon to be assassinated. No, not POTUS; me! Besides the special positive qualities I must have had (though these qualities were unclear to me), apparently another special quality I possessed (which was very clear to me) was being expertly mischievous. So one fateful day, Miss Kaminetsky, in front of the whole class mind you, told me I would no longer be permitted to hold the office of class president. How humiliating! No kidding, it was a terrible thing. I was very ashamed to go home and tell my parents and then to have to return to class in the days to follow and face my classmates. In case you're wondering how my parents reacted, I honestly can't remember, so it must have not been a big deal to them. It is said that travail grows character. Believe me, I was already growing into quite a character.

Chapter 11

Fun and . . . *Nuclear Attacks?*

Public School #105 (P.S.105), was the educational and social center of our neighborhood. I guess there weren't many creative minds in the public education world in New York City because all the K-6 elementary schools were identified by numbers, not names.

P.S. 105 was a four story, pink and tan brick building in a pattern similar to hundreds of other K-6 public schools in New York City. The school occupied about one-half of a large city block bordered by Cruger Avenue, Brady Avenue, and Holland Avenue. I lived on Cruger Avenue directly across the street from P.S. 105. The other important thing about P.S. 105 was the schoolyard, the large cement gathering place which occupied half the school property.

For city kids like us, between the ages of around eight and when we eventually left home as adults, the schoolyard was our playground and social center. In retrospect I suppose that it resembled a prison exercise yard. Every square inch of ground consisted of large gray cement squares with high chain link fencing on all four sides, the east side of which had the fencing mounted on top of an eight foot cement wall. The reason for the high wall on the east side was the difference in grading between Cruger Avenue on the west and Holland Avenue on the east.

The cement wall on the Holland side was used as the backboard to play "Lefty Grove," a stickball variation that involved just two players. I don't know why it was called Lefty Grove, who was a famous left-handed major league baseball pitcher in the 1930s. There were certainly other great baseball pitchers, but the Lefty Grove designation was the common name for this game. Stickball was a major deal for city boys who had limited access to grass and dirt play areas.

In Lefty Grove, one of the two players pitched from a line in the cement which represented the pitcher's mound about 60 feet from the batter. The "bat" was the straightest wooden broomstick handle that one could buy at Ben's Hardware Store on Lydig Avenue, the commercial heart of the neighborhood, just a block from the schoolyard. The ball was a "Hi-Bounce Spaulding," a hard, pink rubber ball, a bit smaller than a regulation size baseball. (We called a regulation size baseball a "hardball," to distinguish it from a "softball"). Are you getting all this? Whatever. The Spauldings, which in Bronxese we called "Spaldeens," were also bought at Ben's Hardware Store, and we would bounce many of them on the store's wooden floor to find the liveliest one to buy, or we got kicked out of the store for annoying other customers, whichever occurred first. Spaldeens were frequently lost by being hit into inaccessible places, or rolling down the many sewer system drains built into the street curbs at frequent intervals. I imagine that there are millions of Spaldeens floating forever in the New York City sewer system.

The object of Lefty Grove was the same as baseball: whoever scores the most runs wins. The pitcher was also the umpire. This made for many lively debates during the game. The "catcher" was the cement wall. An unhit pitch would simply rebound off the wall and bounce back to the pitcher. The ball was soft enough that there was no need to wear a baseball glove. Pitching was overhand just like regular baseball. Only one out was allowed per at-bat. If a ball was hit on the fly and caught by the pitcher, that was an out. If a grounder was fielded without bobbling the ball that was an out, and of course a strikeout was a strikeout.

Sometimes we would hit the Spaldeen hard enough for it to clear the rooftop of the six-story apartment building at the north end of the schoolyard. This was a pretty good shot and must be a 300 foot fly ball. Man it felt great to do this! Then we'd have to retrieve the ball by walking across the length of the schoolyard, down the steps to Cruger Avenue, into the adjacent apartment building, taking the elevator to the sixth floor, then walking up a stairway from the sixth floor to the roof access, hunting all over the roof, get the ball, and make the return trip. We got a lot of exercise playing stickball. The superintendent of the building didn't like us up on his roof, for obvious safety reasons, and would chase us when he caught us up there. Every building had a live-in superintendent who we called "the super."

Let's step back a notch in the timeline for just a moment because the following memory popped into my consciousness. Once a week there was an all-student assembly day in the P.S. 105 auditorium. Boys were required to wear white shirts and green ties and it was referred to as "Middy Day," though I still have no idea what that means. Even

Google doesn't know! We would pledge allegiance to the flag (including "One nation under God"), sing songs, and hear an address from the principal. Sounds kinda like a Hitler youth rally, but I don't recall our principal, Miss Goodwin, having a mustache, or wearing a sidearm.

In the late 1940s and 1950s the Cold War was in full swing. There was widespread belief that a nuclear attack on the U.S.A. by the Russians might actually occur. In school we would have regular unannounced air raid drills. When the alarm sounded we would rush to hide under our desks to be protected in case of an attack. This was not a fun thing; it was scary. In retrospect a very dumb exercise. Think about it: A wooden desk with a writing surface about two feet square and an inch thick was supposed to protect us from nuclear incineration? Duh!

When the old school desks were being replaced at P.S. 105 they were discarded by the truckload. My parents asked me if I wanted one, which I did. They grabbed one and I had it in our home for many years. Our kids enjoyed using it to store their crayons and drawing paper inside the compartment that was hidden under the hinged top. It was a wonderful memento of my grade school years. When our kids were in grade school and we went to open houses at their schools to meet their teachers, we often sat in little chairs, at small desks, not unlike the ones I sat in as a kid attending P.S. 105.

Chapter 12

B.T. and B.C.

Before television and before cable—yes, that's correct—I said before television and before cable. Without TV folks listened to radio programs for home entertainment. My family had a large console-style radio. It stood about three feet high and 18 inches wide in a beautiful dark wooden cabinet. It was powered by electricity and had many different sized electronic glass tubes that could be clearly seen if you turned the radio around and looked into its fully exposed backside. The back of the cabinet was open so that the heat generated by the tubes could dissipate. The tubes were anywhere from two inches to four inches in height and an inch or two in diameter, and they plugged in vertically with a set of metal male prongs that fit matching female socket holes in the base of the radio. Occasionally a tube would burn out and require replacement, which was easy to do without calling a repair person. There was a parts shop nearby that carried replacement tubes.

There were many programs on the radio. I had favorite shows on different nights of the week. There was: "The Lone Ranger"; "The Green Hornet"; "Amos and Andy"; "Baby Snooks"; "Burns and Allen";

and many others. All of it was wholesome family entertainment. There were no such thing as content ratings for radio shows, and no radio shockjocks. There was no need or demand for them.

We got our first TV set when I was around eight or nine years old. It was one of the first TVs in our apartment building. All TVs at the time had small screens. Our TV had a ten inch screen encased in a wood cabinet that sat on a stand that placed the screen at eye level. Of course, the 'color' was black and white. To ensure decent reception, we had a large antenna mounted on the roof of the building hard-wired to our TV. This was a do-it-yourself job involving clamping the metal pole antennae to a chest-high wall on the roof of the building, dropping the antenna wire from the roof to our apartment window, then running the wire from the window into the apartment to the TV. Lots of folks did this and the roof of our building soon looked like a sea of antennas.

Many of the TV shows at the time were broadcast live. Often on so-called "variety" shows (singers, dancers, comedians, interviews), you never knew what might happen if a performer messed up. There was a lot of ad libbing. Often it was hilarious. As time went on there were filmed TV shows, many of which mimicked the earlier radio shows, and many were westerns such as "The Lone Ranger", "Roy Rogers", "Gene Autry", and "Hopalong Cassidy". Other favorites of mine were "Sky King" (a hero who flew an airplane called "The Songbird"), "Captain Video and The Video Ranger" (an outer space adventure series), "Flash Gordon" (another outer space adventure show), "Howdy Doody" (a string puppet show with a live studio audience of children), and "Kookla, Fran & Ollie" (a hand puppet show like the Muppets), to name just a few.

There were no late evening TV shows, and programming often ended on all channels by 9:00 or 10:00 pm. Until morning cartoons became the rage for children there weren't any daytime shows either. I know what some of you are thinking? "What planet was I raised on?" It really was planet Earth.

Often my friends and I would go to a movie matinee to escape the heat and high humidity of the city in July and August. We had two movie theaters within walking distance, the RKO Pelham, and the Globe. A matinee in the 1950s cost 25 cents, for which we got to see several cartoons, a newsreel, a serial, and a feature length movie.

"Serials" were movies shown in chapters. At a Saturday matinee serials usually ran just a few minutes and preceded the feature film. My favorite serial was "Tarzan". To see the next chapter you had to return to the movie theater the following week. Every chapter ended with a: "they'll-never-get-out of-this-one" moment. Lots of fun!

I was shaped largely by wonderful women in my life. My grandmother, Sarah, who was my mother's mother, and Sarah's sister, my maiden aunt Rosie, lived on Wallace Avenue just two blocks east of our building. Though it was very unusual during this era my grandmother and her husband, my grandfather Harry, were separated. I don't remember how long they were separated, or the reason they were separated, but they didn't live together at any time during my life. Grandpa Harry was very kind to me and visited us regularly. He was quite a character.

My mom, who was grandpa Harry's favorite of his three daughters, told me that he would take her along when he went to play cards with his friends and dressed her up in her nicest clothes to show her off to his buddies. This is where mom learned to play cards which she enjoyed playing throughout her life. Mom told me that grandpa Harry often thought that he was being followed and would wear disguises and take circuitous travel routes to throw off the people following him. He worked as a steelworker and was small-framed but very strong and wiry.

When I was around 10 years old a wonderful ritual began between me and my grandma Sarah and aunt Rosie. Every Sunday morning I would ride my balloon-tired Schwinn bike up the hill on Brady Avenue to my grandma's apartment to have breakfast with her and aunt Rosie. She would let me drink coffee—actually it was milk with just enough coffee added to make it taste coffeeish—and with it I would have matzoh with butter and fresh farmer's cheese. We'd chat about this and that for a while, then grandma would give me a quarter and I'd leave making a beeline for the candy store on the corner of Wallace and Brady where I would buy a Hershey candy bar for a nickel and pocket the remaining 20 cents for a rainy day. Then I'd zip back home down the hill on my bike. This was a very special Sunday event for me for years. Grandma Sarah was a wonderful, loving, and kind woman.

She may be the person responsible for my addiction to chocolate. Thanks grandma!

Living close to the Bronx Zoo, one of the finest and largest zoos in the world, was a special part of the area of the Bronx where I lived with my parents and brother. As a family we visited the zoo often. When I was old enough to spend most of my outdoor time with friends rather than with mom and dad, I was bound to eventually get into more trouble. One of the troubling events—at least it was troubling for my parents—was a day when some friends and I were at the Bronx Zoo and somehow got locked in after the main gates were closed. We were able to find a way out but by the time I got home, much later than expected, my parents were frantic. They were about to call the police. I can't remember the punishment that was inflicted upon me for turning their hair noticeably grayer from worry, but I know that they were more relieved than they were angry. Lucky for me.

Bicycles were a way of life for us city kids and a great form of exercise. My friends and I spent many hours up and down the streets of our neighborhood on our bikes. There was also a wonderful bicycle path that ran from near our home to perhaps six miles north along the eastern edge of Bronx Park, paralleling the Bronx River. We loved to pedal up and down this route through a beautiful wooded area just a stone's throw from the endless density of apartment buildings visible just through the trees.

Chapter 13

Jr. High and High School

After graduating from elementary school, based on my high scores on a test that all students were required to take, I was placed into a new education program in the New York City public school system called "Special Progress", which became known as "SP". The SP program was designed for qualifying students to take three years of work in two years. In other words, we were accelerated through seventh, eighth, and ninth grades in two rather than three years. I'm not clear at all on what the hurry was, but my parents thought it was a good idea and signed me up. In retrospect, it was ill-conceived and later discontinued.

I didn't find the SP program to be unusually difficult academically. However, two significant and unexpected results of the program were: 1) I had to travel by subway to the SP school, which was a few subway stops north of my neighborhood. There were only two or three SP classes at this school, Olinville Junior High School, the majority of classes being regular seventh and eighth grade classes. There were around 1500 students at Olinville, in a predominantly Italian neighborhood, much different from my home neighborhood which was 95% Jewish. Not that you couldn't be Italian and Jewish, but that was not typically the case. The regular junior high kids resented the "SPs" being in their school. We were often harassed, sometimes violently. This was more of an educational experience than any of us expected. 2) As a result of the acceleration academically, after we graduated we were integrated into regular high school as sophomores rather than as freshmen. Academically this wasn't a big deal. Socially it was a very big deal. We SPs were sophomores, but we were a year younger than all the other sophomores. This was especially difficult socially. Girls mature faster than boys, and we had a difficult time trying to fit in with girls at our grade level who were on average a year older. One year may not seem like a significant age difference, but at 14 and 15 years of age the differences between boys and girls is sizable. In addition, the sophomores were all freshman together the year before and had formed their cliques that were hard for us to break into.

Yet there are definitely some fond memories of Olinville Junior High School. Here's a few.

Mr. Garafolo. A P.E. teacher who was a heart-throb for the girls. He also taught a dance class that both boys and girls were required to take. This was a class that I hated. I still remember one especially beautiful girl, not an SP, (unless SP stood for Sexy Person) that Mr. Garafolo frequently chose to demonstrate dance steps. Whenever I saw her in the school cafeteria I couldn't take my eyes off her. She was slender, shapely, and graceful, with straight dark hair to her shoulders, and long, straight-cut bangs down to her eyebrows. I can't remember her name but I remember the nickname I gave her: "The Doll."

Then there was feisty Miss Donelin, my English teacher. She was amazing! I'll never forget her confrontation with the toughest kid in the school, Rocco LoBosco. No, I'm not making up his name, it was really Rocco LoBosco. Rocco was a gang leader and God only knows what he was into. On this memorable day he was outside our classroom making a racket. Miss Donelin opened the classroom door, looked up into his face, which was about two heads above hers, gave him a firm reprimand, and then told him to get lost—I loosely paraphrase. He went away without a whimper. Miss Donelin was my hero from that day forward. By the way, she was also a great teacher.

Rita. I can't remember her last name but I'll never forget Rita. Rita was Rocco's girlfriend. Rita and Rocco, sounds like a movie title. Rita was a total knockout. Tall, long blond hair, and far more shapely than any junior high schooler had a right to be. She caused many young boys' jaws to drop open anytime she was within sight. The image of a junior high school Marilyn Monroe jumps into my mind. One morning Rita came to a school assembly in the auditorium and walked in wearing a see-through blouse with no bra. What a shock! What a treat for us guys! At least for the brief few moments it lasted. Here again, Miss Donelin, the fiery faculty terror, intercepted Rita and in no uncertain terms told her to go home and change and never to come to school dressed (undressed?) like that again. Rita complied. The school assembly was in shambles. The memory is tatooed into my mind with a big smile.

Based on my experience as an SP, I spent three years at Christopher Columbus High School, my sophomore through senior years, graduating in 1958. The school had about 3000 students. High school was not very challenging for me academically. I studied as little as possible and my grades were decent enough. The school, believe it or not, in the heart of New York City, had a rifle team which was considered a varsity sport on an equal level with all other varsity sports.

I tried out for the rifle team and made the cut. The team coach was the school Librarian, Mr. Dunn. It seemed funny to me that a librarian would be a rifle team coach, sort of a non sequitor. He was a pleasant, soft-spoken gentleman, and a good coach. The school had a very fine rifle team that competed well against other high schools throughout New York City frequently winning our Bronx Division title. We practiced live firing at Fort Schuyler, a U.S. Navy base on the bay in a remote part of The Bronx, that permitted us to use their indoor firing range.

I remember during one fateful team practice when we were giving tryouts to hopefuls, that I was almost shot. After firing was finished the paper targets were retrieved for scoring by walking out onto the range and bringing them back to the scorer. Before this could occur there had to be assurance that all rifles were set aside with their bolts open. The shooting stations were narrow booths with thin plywood floor-to-ceiling partitions between them. I had been shooting with a rookie in the booth immediately to my left. He forgot to open the bolt of his rifle when he firmly planted it on the concrete floor to lean it in the corner of his booth. His rifle, with the bolt in firing position, containing a live round, went off, firing the bullet through the partition into my booth somewhere into the ceiling just above me. I was covered with wood splinters but the bullet missed me. It was so frightening that I shook with fear, followed by considerable anger. This rookie did not make the team. As you might imagine, safety was an enormously important issue especially for high schoolers who were firing live ammunition. A .22 caliber bullet has a range of more than one mile. These were not toys. Before any of us were permitted to load a bullet we were deeply indoctrinated in safety training.

In my senior year I was elected Captain of the rifle team and was very proud to have earned that honor. That year we also competed for the New York City championship against an outstanding team from Brooklyn Technical High School. We lost the gold by 13 points . . . 13 out of 1000. That's only a 1.3% difference! This was very disappointing for me, much more so because one of our shooters, perhaps our best, had missed practice recently and had a subpar score at this championship competition. I still feel the disappointment, after so many years have passed, when I think about how one team member made such a big difference because he didn't work to consistently do his best.

Chapter 14

Summer Camp

A special benefit of being a member of my high school rifle team was the opportunity to get a summer job as a rifle instructor at coach Dunn's summer camp. Mr. Dunn offered me this opportunity in my senior year and I accepted with great excitement. I'd be able to do a lot of shooting during the summer with someone else providing the rifle and paying for the ammunition. It was my first opportunity to be away from home for an extended period of time.

The camp was called Balfour Lake Camp, a boys' camp on a small lake from which the camp got its name. The camp included boys between the ages of six and twelve who for a glorious eight weeks got to live away from home in rustic wooden log cabins, sleep in bunk beds, share bathroom facilities, participate in all kinds of planned activities, and eat together in a large dining hall three times a day. The camp was located in a microscopically small town, North Creek, New York, in the densely and beautifully forested Adirondack Mountains. Better known destinations such as Lake George and Saratoga Springs, New

York, were an hour away by car. I made some good friends among the other counselors during this memorable summer.

Just as you might find in a coming-of-age movie, across the lake was, you probably guessed it, a girls' camp. Other than on weekends and nights off we only got reasonably close to the girl counselors while we were on duty at the lake while the campers were swimming. Sometimes we'd swim or canoe a bit closer but only close enough to wave and check out the merchandise from a distance. Of course the girls were doing the same thing.

During time off in the evenings we would often walk about a half mile up the narrow, dark road, using flashlights to see where we were going, to meet and greet members of the opposite sex at a place halfway between the two camps, called "The Lair", where they served snacks, sandwiches, nonalcoholic drinks, and played recorded music. I learned from the more experienced counselors that the first time at The Lair each camp season was when guys and gals paired off for the summer. It was like a once-a-year sales event; better get there early to have the pick of the lot! I didn't believe it at first, but sure enough, that's exactly what happened. During my first trip to The Lair I connected with a girl named Cassie. This was a period in time when Susan and I were not yet in a serious relationship so I was free to sample. Cassie was a very attractive, well-bred, and intelligent girl. We dated exclusively for the first half of the summer. We kissed a lot but Cassie wouldn't allow me to get to second base, which was frustrating as I saw my buddies making more progress with their girlfriends. With mutual agreement Cassie and I ended our relationship.

Shortly thereafter I went to a social with my friends. The girls' camp girls were there in force and most were coupled off as I had expected. As I watched the couples dancing, an especially beautiful girl grabbed my attention. She was olive complexioned with gorgeous long, straight black hair, and a stunning figure. She could have passed for Native American. Much to my amazement, on two occasions while she was on the dance floor I thought that she winked at me. It must have been my imagination. She was with her boyfriend so it couldn't be real. Then one of the girls came up to me and said that the girl whose eyes met mine was breaking up with her boyfriend that night and she was interested in getting to know me. I was astonished! This kind of thing just didn't happen to me. Her name was Joan and I was told that she was waiting outside, if I was interested. *Are you kidding?* A gorgeous girl, interested in me, a healthy, normal, 17 year old guy without a girlfriend? What's there to not be interested in!

Joan and I became a couple for the rest of the summer. She lived in the Bronx not far from where I lived and we dated for a while after our summer together. I had strong feelings for Joan and as had been the case with every girlfriend I ever had, I wanted the relationship to be exclusive. I guess I was always looking for a mate rather than a fling. Sadly for me Joan didn't feel ready to commit to one guy and so I told her that because we felt so differently we probably should not see each other any more. I never saw her or heard from her again. I've thought of her often over the years. She was intelligent and refined, in addition to being beautiful and fun to be with. I greatly enjoyed her friendship and companionship while it lasted.

Once or twice during my summer as a camp counselor a few of us would take a bus to Lake George, a very popular tourist location.

The lake was truly spectacular. On one visit to Lake George I bought a Bowie knife. We'd heard rumors that there were wild bears seen in the vicinity of The Lair. Buying the large knife was rationalized as something that I needed for personal protection. Really, I just liked it. It had deer horn handles and came in a beautiful full leather sheath that could be worn on a belt. I actually wore it to The Lair . . . made me feel like a frontiersman ready to take on a bear if I had to. Yeah, right.

One night while a few of us were walking back to camp from The Lair we heard a rustling sound in the woods up ahead. It stopped us in our tracks. First thought: A bear! As we made our way forward in the pitch dark with our flashlights shining hopelessly anemic beams of light, when we got about halfway back to camp, the rustling sound became much louder. Without having to say a word to each other we simultaneously broke into a dead run toward camp fueled by a considerable amount of adrenaline. Did I ever pull my Bowie knife to make ready to fight the vicious wild beast that was obviously stalking us? Heck no! I ran for my life. We informed the camp officials of our experience and they contacted the Forest Service who set humane traps for the bear, which was soon caught. It was a Black Bear, around 200 pounds, which was trucked to a more remote location and set free unharmed.

It was in July of this summer at Balfour Lake Camp, 1959, that I turned 18 and was required by law to register for the U.S. Army draft that existed at the time and which continued for many more years. To register in a timely manner with the closest Draft Board I had to take a one hour bus ride to Saratoga Springs, the home of a world-famous horse racing track. Men were deemed eligible to be drafted until age 35 as long as they were physically fit. When I graduated college in June 1963, I was notified to report to take a mandatory U.S. Army physical exam at Whitehall Street in Manhattan. This was the largest military induction center in the country. Not a fun experience. I was classified "1-A", which was the rating given to those most fit to serve in the military. Prime beef. The war in Viet Nam was heating up. Not the best time in history to be ripe for the picking. Susan and I were married in October 1963, and married men were exempt from the draft. Later, as the war ground on and became bigger, exemptions for married men were discontinued, however, if a married man had children, he was exempt. We had our first child in 1966, and so I was one step ahead of the draft until 1976, when I turned 35 and was no longer eligible based on age. These years during which I was potentially eligible to be involuntarily inducted into the military and shipped off to war were not the most comfortable years of my life. Ironically, before Susan and I were married, I was seriously considering a military career as an Air Force officer. Both my parents and Susan's parents talked me out of it. Just one of many big decisions made at life's frequent crossroads. Further irony: Our oldest son, Eric, joined the U.S. Air Force when he was 18 and retired after 24 years of service, including serving in the Middle East during the first Gulf War.

The summer camp experience was a blast in spite of Mel, the senior counselor, who was a total jackass. Any time he could stop our fun and games he did so. We hated him. On the last day of camp as we all waited for the busses to arrive to take us back to New York City, a few friends and I decided to rebel. The kids were supposed to be in their cabins preparing to leave and the counselors were told that they too must remain in their cabins. A few of us, bored with the inactivity, wanted to toss a football around and when we stepped outside our cabins the head counselor got all bent out of shape. We ignored him, ridiculed him, and kept tossing the ball around. He stormed off and reported us to the owner, Max Dunn, my high school rifle team coach, who had given me this great summer job opportunity. To make an example of us to the other staff, Mr. Dunn fired us! (I'm sure that we also pushed his buttons to the point where he had no alternative.) On the last day of camp! Furthermore, he did not permit us to return home on the busses with the rest of the camp. Though I was embarrassed that I'd disappointed my coach, it was really a very funny episode. So the four of us who were fired returned to New York in Danny's convertible, with the top down, on a beautiful late August day. A lot more fun than a four hour bus ride packed with a bunch of crazed young boys.

Chapter 15

Real World Lessons

My favorite line from the movie "The Princess Bride" is the masked man's response when he is dueling with Inigo Montoya, and Inigo desperately says: "I must know who you are!" The masked man's simply stated reply is:

"Get used to disappointment."

From about fifth grade until I got my first paying job in high school, my parents gave me a small cash allowance every week. It wasn't much but it helped teach me to be responsible with money, plan expenditures, and save. I loved saving to buy gifts for my mother because she was always so appreciative of anything that I got for her. She taught me the joy of giving and to this day I love to search for just the right gift for others.

Another summer job, which I'd gotten through a friend of a friend of a friend was a bittersweet experience. It was in the garment district in midtown Manhattan, so I took the subway from the Bronx to my job every day, often in sweltering, humid, typical New York City summer weather. It was about a 40 minute ride on subway cars that had yet to be air conditioned. No place was more hot and humid during the summer months than a steel train car riding the rails underground through the labyrinth of the New York City subway system.

I worked for a women's clothing manufacturer named Henry Rosenthal, who was an eccentric figure. He wore red socks every day with navy blue suits, some said because he cemented a lucrative business deal in the past while wearing such an outfit. I helped to maintain inventory, opening boxes of merchandise and hanging them on display racks. The showroom was open to the public and part of my job was to help customers. Business slowed down and so I was laid off halfway through the summer. It was too late to find another summer job and so I was at loose ends for the rest of the summer.

My life lesson: the reality of the working-person is often unpredictable and sometimes grim.

I believe that this not-so-dreadful-in-the-scheme-of-things experience heavily influenced my course of study in college. I majored in Human Resources with a minor in Labor Economics. My future plan was a career path that would permit me to try to influence the relationship between employers and employees in a positive way. I spent a 43 year career doing just that.

Ginger

When I was 13 years old and my brother was 8, dad surprised us by bringing home a Cocker Spaniel puppy that we named "Ginger" because of her color. It was partly my responsibility to walk our dog—no simple matter when you live on the fifth floor of an apartment building, and especially during the winters in New York City. Nonetheless, this didn't bother me much and it added to my lessons in responsibility. Ginger was a good companion and playmate for me and my brother, Edward.

When Spaldeens were beaten to death playing stickball they would often split in half along the center seam. Ginger especially liked to chase balls and loved to play with half a Spaldeen that she'd chew on and hold in her mouth with the concave side facing her so that it kind of looked like a large, pink stick-on nose. She would tug hard and growl if you tried to pry it from her jaws, but her tail wagged like crazy. This was a game that she loved. She also became quite adept at catching the half Spaldeen on the fly. We had Ginger for 13 years. She was put down because she had advanced cancer and was suffering. I vividly remember going with my father to our Vet, Dr. Fletcher, for Ginger to be 'put to sleep'. The Dr. gently placed her on a table and gave her an injection. I remember asking him how long it would take, and he replied that she was already gone. It was instantaneous and I believe painless. This was the only humane thing to do, though it was difficult to witness.

My life lesson: Death is part of life and it hurts to lose a loved one.

How Do Guys Survive?
(Or: Dumb Things I Did and Lived to Tell About.)

One of the things that I was able to do very well was throw hard, far, and accurately. No matter what the shape of the projectile, as long as it fit in my hand, I could throw it well. This skill gave me an edge because a strong, accurate throwing arm got me selected to play pick-up games and earned me a place as a defending center fielder, my choice position. Few runners tried to take extra bases when I was in center field.

I don't believe that this skill is an innate characteristic that a person is born able to do well. It is a cultivated skill. Don't laugh, it's true. The way it is cultivated is by throwing stuff . . . often and regularly. In the winters in New York City, throwing stuff was a natural pastime after snowfalls. Snowballs. The weapon of choice for young boys on the streets of the city. We would be out early in the day testing the snow to see how well it would pack because to throw a snowball hard and accurately it had to be perfectly formed. To perfectly form a snowball, an art form in itself, the snow has to be a bit wet so that it could be shaped without crumbling, and then thrown hard without disintegrating in mid-flight. Of course a hard-packed slightly wet snowball hits the target harder. All the better.

So, here are a bunch of young guys practicing their snowball crafts, scanning the streets for targets of opportunity. The easiest targets of opportunity were . . . girls! Any girls. They were practice targets with no risk attached. They'd scream and run, but, they didn't return fire. I know, it sounds cowardly, right? Hogwash. It was a crude form of courtship. We were too young to approach girls with charm, so we made contact by showing them our prowess with snowballs. OK, so maybe I made the last part up. It was just plain fun, and no one really got hurt. And the girls expected it. Sometimes any kind of attention is better than none.

When we got bored bombarding girls with snowballs, we'd choose up sides, each group usually across the street from one another, using the lines of parked cars for cover. Then we'd start launching snowballs. There wasn't really any scorekeeping. Each guy just tried to hit as many other guys as possible until our fingers were numb from the cold, or we were too tired to continue. There might be a few bruises that resulted, especially if someone was hit in the head, but for the most part this was benign fun and good exercise. This was where my throwing arm was cultivated. I loved to throw!

When I was a bit older a more dangerous and fortunately less frequent throwing activity came into the picture.

The P.S. 105 schoolyard was directly across the street from the building where I lived. On the next street east of the schoolyard in the 1950s was a large, empty lot, about half a city block in size, virgin land with heavy brush, small hills, and large boulders. I can tell you right now, you will think that I was an idiot to get involved in the following "game" with other boys in the neighborhood.

The empty lot was a magnet for young guys. We could play hide and seek, cops and robbers, or whatever we could imagine to do in this convenient, wild, unsupervised playground in our congested Bronx neighborhood. One of our "games" was rock fights. We'd choose up sides, usually only two or three on a side. Then we'd collect small rocks, seek cover among the boulders, and then start throwing rocks at each other. I know, I know, sounds like the children of cavemen going wild. It was a completely nutsy thing to do. Fortunately, wounds were minor, but someone could have been seriously injured. By the way, we never told our parents about this particular game which we really didn't 'play' very often.

Within a few years our empty lot disappeared under two new apartment buildings that were built on the site. It was no surprise that such prime real estate would not remain untouched for very long. Sadly, our little badlands playground went away.

The Standoff

I was a college freshman at Boston University at the age of 17. As I mentioned earlier I was in an accelerated junior high school program where we did three years work in two years.

At B.U. it was my first time away from home except for the one summer that I was a camp counselor in upstate New York. College away from home was a big deal for me. I shared a two-bedroom suite with two roommates. We drew straws for the single bedroom and I won. The mens' dormitory I lived in was called Myles Standish Hall, and was on Bay State Road, just a few blocks from the Charles River, with Harvard University and M.I.T. sticking their noses up at us from the other side of the river. We used to say that Harvard wasn't really a university, it was an attitude.

The dorm was large, housing several hundred young men, and we had a lot of fun. I became friendly with a group of guys on my floor several of whom roomed together down the hall. We'd drift back and forth to each other's rooms to just shoot the breeze or sometimes study together. One of them, Neil Thompson, was in the same academic program I was, so I knew him best. Neil was a fun guy and a good friend. He had a special talent that I never witnessed anyone else performing either before I met him, or anytime in my life since. Neil could fart on command. I kid you not. So, any time someone would point to Neil, he could and would muster up a fart. Could this have been a genetic gift? Was he of a rare species of human beings who could control body functions that others could not? Who cares; it was just incredibly funny. He was very proud of his unique talent which I'm sure got him many dates with hot chicks.

During my residence at Myles Standish Hall I did one of the all-time dumbest things I've ever done in my life. I was visiting with Neil and his roommates in their room. One of them who I wasn't especially friendly with was Bruce Boodleman. I can still picture his dumb face and crewcut hair as clear as day.

We were messing around in the room while Bruce was allegedly studying, and he asked us several times to keep the noise down. Not an unreasonable request. As usual everyone ignored him. This went on for a while, with me intentionally increasing the distraction just to piss him off. Pushing people's hot buttons was a specialty of mine. I was truly very gifted in this way. What happened next was almost surreal.

Bruce suddenly came at me from behind grabbing me around my chest with one hand. He was half a head taller than I was and had a significant weight advantage. With his other hand he put a knife blade to my throat!

Everyone in the room immediately froze in their tracks. You could hear the proverbial pin drop, and possibly the sounds of guys soiling their underwear. Bruce, who was very agitated, then said to me: "If you don't get out my room right now I'm going to hurt you." I didn't move or struggle. I knew that Bruce was an asshole (everyone knew this, and of course he was now proving it live and in living color, in front of three witnesses), but I was also convinced that he was a bigmouthed coward. I did not believe that he intended to, or had the guts, to cut my throat, or, for that matter, cut me in any way. He was bluffing and just shooting off his big, dumb mouth. So, while everyone was still in freeze-frame mode, with looks of horror on their faces, I said to Bruce: "The only way you'll get me to leave this room is feet first." Brilliant move, huh?

Not a sound was uttered for what was probably 10 or 15 seconds, which seemed more like 10 or 15 minutes. Then, Bruce released his grip, lowered the knife and moved away from me. I then said goodbye to my friends, turned, slowly made my way to the door, and left, returning to my own room, where I contemplated the magnificent act of bravery that I had displayed . . . at the possible risk of my life.

At that moment I might have exceeded Bruce Boodleman's firm hold on "The World's Dumbest Shit" title, at least temporarily. A little while later, the other two guys from Bruce's room came down the hall to tell me what an amazing thing I'd done by calling Bruce's bluff and making a bigger fool of him than he already was. One of them told me that when Bruce released his hold on me I should have beat the crap out of him. It wasn't necessary. Bruce beat the crap out of himself more completely than I could ever have done. Bruce later came to my room and apologized for what he'd done. I accepted his apology. Of course I never wrote home about this to my parents; as I said, I only held "The World's Dumbest Shit" title for a very brief time, happy to relinquish it back to Bruce Boodleman.

Weapons of Less Destruction

Firecrackers are hardly weapons of mass destruction and certainly not the most exciting explosive devices in the grand scheme of things. Hollywood special effects gurus are now able to create in their studios realistic visual portrayals of heart pounding disasters—hurricanes, earthquakes, volcanoes, tornados, tsunamis, nuclear holocausts, and battlefield mayhem—for viewers to gasp at while sipping wine in their living rooms.

Yet, to a couple of 18 year old guys, high on naturally produced testosterone, and bent on excitement, the prospect of getting our hands on firecrackers was exciting and very tempting. The only problem was that buying, selling, or igniting firecrackers within the limits of New York City was illegal for private citizens. But, anywhere something is illegal, there's a black market able to find it, get it, and sell it. This is the American way!

As noted earlier I was a well-behaved kid, really and truly, except for the propensity in my younger years to beat the crud out of other kids just for the heck of it. I never maimed anyone other than inflicting scrapes and bruises, and I only used something other than my bare hands one time, and that was purely in self-defense. Since the statute of limitations is probably up on this 'crime', if the aforementioned statute of limitations ever even applied to eight year olds, I can now confess this event with impunity.

It was winter in New York City and we'd had an unusually large snowfall. The Department of Sanitation plows had left a large mound of snow on the corner of our street. A perfect mountaintop for eight year olds to conquer.

My next door neighbor's son, my best friend Joey, who was a year older than me, decided that he wanted me to yield the mountaintop to him. We were busily shoveling snow right next to each other, packed tight in our padded snowsuits that kept us warm but seriously slowed down our movement, kinda like the pics of astronauts in puffy spacesuits moving in slow motion in weightless environments.

Anyway, we both got heated—figuratively and literally—and Joey made the mistake of lifting his shovel to take a whack at me, and I was just quicker on the draw. My faster-than-a-speeding-bullet shovel split his head open. Like I said, pure self-defense.

After a few hysterics and some stitches, Joey and I were buds again. Many years later, after we'd not seen each other in maybe 30 years, Susan arranged for a surprise lunch meeting with Joey while she and I were celebrating our wedding anniversary in L.A. The first thing that Joey said to me when we met outside a restaurant in Marina del Rey was: "You didn't bring a shovel, did you?" Joey was at this time divorced and living on his boat at the marina. I couldn't help wondering if his life choices might have turned out differently if I hadn't scrambled his brain a bit. Oh well. He that lives by the shovel dies by the shovel . . . or something like that.

Firecrackers; that's where this started, right? At the time my best friend was Jack Green. Both of us liked playing ball, and this was our original connection. Jack and I had very different personalities. I tended to play by the rules. He didn't, if he could get away with it. And get away with it he often did. He had uncanny luck getting out of trouble. I wasn't a weak-willed person, but I was usually content letting others take the lead as long as I didn't have any especially strong objections to how to spend the day, decide what movie to see, whether to go for a bike ride or play ball, eat deli or Chinese . . . that kind of thing.

Jack liked living on the edge and was an accomplished schemer. Sometimes I lived a life of danger through and with Jack. He wasn't my hero, he was my alter ego, the engine of my vicarious existence.

Somehow, as only he could, Jack located someone who would sell him illegal firecrackers. It was to be a carefully staged transaction, for cash of course, in a Bronx location that was outside of our typical stomping grounds. Jack asked me to go with him to get the firecrackers. I agreed because it sounded exciting and I'd never have done something like this on my own.

The plan, which Jack had worked out on the phone with the seller, was as follows. We would arrive at a specific address at an arranged time. The seller was to have hidden the contraband fireworks in a covered garbage can placed on the specified street corner. We were instructed to put a paper bag with the money in the garbage can, in plain sight, while at the same time retrieving the package of fireworks from the can. Of course this put us at a big disadvantage. First, we were in unfamiliar territory. Second, it wasn't the best neighborhood in the Bronx. Third, we'd be on foot at the most critical time, while making the deposit and pickup. And fourth, not knowing what our seller looked like, he and perhaps other cronies of his could have been stationed close by to double-cross us by taking our money, beating the crud out of us, and keeping the fireworks.

Now, Jack liked the thrill of the danger, but he was not stupid. I didn't know until we were on our way to the meeting place that Jack had already taken all these risk factors into account by previously scouting the rendezvous location. He clearly didn't like the odds but he really wanted the fireworks. To even the odds a bit, and much to my shock, he brought along a gun! Where the hell did he get a gun? Would he actually use it if things got dicey? Thank God it never came to that. He kept the gun concealed in his coat pocket while we followed the instructions to the letter, and the transaction came off without a hitch. That was a very exciting, risky, and especially stupid little adventure.

Chapter 16

Why Marry?

Why did I want to marry Susan almost 50 years ago?

Aside from a physical attraction that we shared, there was much more to it; there had to be for our relationship to grow for over seven years before we decided to marry.

I suppose the simple answer is that I took a long view of our future lives together. I believe that Susan did the same thing. By this I mean that I purposefully looked far down the path of life and asked myself a few important questions:

1) Did I believe that I loved her? I didn't mean romantically, though I did love her in that way as well. But in the sense that I wanted to be with her and with no one else for the rest of my life. To be soul mates. The answer was: Yes.

2) Did I believe that she loved me as I loved her? The answer was: Yes.

3) Did I believe that she would faithfully and diligently work alongside me to make our marriage as strong and as good as possible in this imperfect world? The answer was: Yes.

4) Did I believe that she would be a good mother to our children? The answer was: Yes.

With the answers to these questions settled in my mind I asked Susan to marry me knowing that her answer would be: Yes.

And so our adventure as husband and wife began in October 1963.

I can't imagine any marriage without difficulties along the way. People are just too imperfect. We certainly had our share of cuts and bruises, and times when we wondered if we were truly meant to be together for our lifetimes. But we weathered these times together and were never at a place where we gave serious thought to ending our marriage or to be separated, even though we may have spoken such cruel thoughts in fits of irrational frustration or anger.

Look at the rate of divorce in our country. According to a variety of sources the likelihood of a first marriage ending in divorce is around 41%. In addition, according to one source, based on age at the time of marriage for divorced individuals, the highest divorce rate is among those who married between 20-24 years of age.

When we were married, Susan was 20 and I was 22, in the age category at highest risk for divorce. Why were Susan and I able to survive our life-storms? I believe that there are a couple of basic yet very important reasons:

1) We got to know each other very well in the seven years before we married. This limits the number of surprises that can arise after getting married. The fewer the number of surprises, the less the likelihood of a surprise that can be fatal to a marriage.

2) We meant the words we said at our wedding. We intended to remain committed to one another for as long as we lived no matter what life threw at us.

And we did, through thick and thin.

A bone of great contention between us throughout our marriage was Susan's smoking. I'd smoked for a few years beginning in college and then for a few years thereafter. There is a Bible verse that states that the sins of the fathers are visited upon their children and sometimes even upon their children's children. This may seem harsh and unjust on the surface, yet as I thought about it, I believe that what it means is that children are heavily influenced by their parent's behaviors and often replicate the behaviors in their own lives, sometimes not even on a conscious level. The result often turns out to be the same as it was for the parents. Everyone in Susan's household smoked. Susan started smoking at 14, and she continued to smoke for over 40 years. Susan's father died following a recurrence of lung cancer. It is certainly likely that her smoking over such a long period of time had a direct bearing on her contracting lung cancer that ultimately ended her life.

Chapter 17

New Beginnings

Our first apartment as husband and wife was in Queens, New York. Queens is one of New York City's five boroughs. The other four boroughs are: Manhattan, Brooklyn, Staten Island, and the Bronx. The little one bedroom, tiny windowless kitchen, one windowless bathroom apartment was our castle. It was in a seven-story building, probably not more than five or six years old, relatively new compared with the buildings we lived in growing up with our families, which were 30 or more years old when we were married.

It was funny to me that in 1963, our rent of $125 per month was more than my parents were paying for their spacious two bedroom, rent-controlled apartment that was built like the Rock of Gibralter, while our place was more like the cardboard box of Gibralter. No matter. It was all ours and we were thrilled. The neighborhood was good, with Kissena Park, the future site of the New York World's Fair, just a few blocks away. It was congested—many apartment buildings, lots of people—but we were accustomed to this kind of environment as native, inner-city New Yorkers.

I had my first job in Human Resources since graduating college that year and was very excited to begin my career. The commute to work was a hassle. Each morning, Monday through Friday, I had to walk a couple of blocks to catch a city bus to the subway station, about a 10 minute ride. Then I took the subway, including one station where I needed to get off and transfer to another subway line. The commute was an hour each way. Not an unusual commute for New Yorkers, but not the easiest way to get to and from work.

I was working in lower Manhattan for a division of Kimberly-Clark Corporation that manufactured envelopes. My work day began at 7:00 am. Therefore, a normal commute of an hour or so required that I get up at 5:00 am to shower, dress, eat, and leave myself a margin for late busses or trains, in order to make it to work on time. You do what you gotta do, right? The good part was that my work day ended at 3:30 pm, so I missed the real New York City rush hour both ways.

I worked for Kimberly-Clark for less than a year when they announced that they were closing the New York facility and merging it into their operations in Ohio, where the division was based. I was the first person to be laid off.

Life lesson: I learned firsthand what it feels like to be handed two weeks pay and walked out the door. This lesson made an indelible imprint on me because it turned out that later in my career I was often called upon to be part of difficult personnel decisions including who should be laid off. Susan was still working at the time as a secretary for an insurance company in Manhattan so we weren't too panicked about my situation.

Within two weeks of my layoff I was hired into a HR position at the corporate offices of the J. C. Penney Company, located near Rockefeller Center, a great location in Manhattan. Penney's had their own 45-story headquarters building with over 2000 employees. This was a wonderful opportunity and over the next five years I learned a lot and progressed in my responsibilities.

Here's a sidebar that to this day is hard for me to believe even though I lived it. The referral for the job at Penney's was through an employment agency that I'd signed up with. The person who hired me at Penney's, who became my mentor and good friend, told me that the employment agency asked him if he truly wanted to interview me because I was Jewish. Here's the deal: 25% of the population of New York City was Jewish! And here's some yo-yo offering to disqualify me because I was Jewish. First, I don't know how he knew so confidently that I was Jewish. It never came up in our screening interview. He certainly didn't ask me if I was circumcised or if Hebrew was my first language. Second, there must have been some tangible reason that the question was asked. I later saw the picture more clearly.

After my first two years at Penney's, during which I worked in the HR office that was responsible for the 2000 people who worked at the New York headquarters, I was promoted to a position with corporate-wide responsibility. This involved a transfer in the building to the 41st floor, where the corporate HR department occupied the entire floor. When I began working on the 41st floor I very soon came to realize that out of about 100 corporate HR employees I was the first and only Jewish employee to become part of the corporate HR staff. Imagine: New York City, with an enormous Jewish population, and I'm the first Jew in the corporate HR department?! Now the pieces came together. The question raised by the employment agency had to do with their understanding that the J. C. Penney Company avoided hiring Jews . . . in New York City! I was floored by this astounding reality.

Life lesson: Anti-Semitism was alive and well even in American Jewish strongholds. Still is.

Chapter 18

Leaving Our Home Turf

My mentor at Penney's left to go to work with an old college buddy of his at a small company called DASA Corporation, located in Andover, Massachusetts. DASA was being drastically reorganized. He called me shortly after he started his job there as V.P. for Administration, and told me that they were completely revamping the company from top to bottom, had never had a HR department, and were offering me the job to join the company and create their HR department from scratch. I felt that this was a remarkable opportunity, but Susan and I were conflicted about leaving New York City, where all our relatives and friends were. We'd never lived outside of New York City. Yet she recognized the opportunity, and said to me that the decision was mine. Our first child was two years old at the time, so there weren't any complications about him leaving his friends, pulling him out of school in the middle of a school term, and so on.

I agonized over this offer for weeks, at one time accepting it, then calling my friend back and retracting my acceptance. I then realized that the security offered by a large corporation like the J. C. Penney

Company, where I was doing well, far outweighed the security, or lack thereof, of a little electronics manufacturing company that had been struggling to survive, with a couple of hundred employees, and with a single physical location in a 100 year old converted textile mill.

Would you like to know what my worst nightmare was? OK, here it is: If 100 of J. C. Penney's stores all burned to the ground on the same day, it would cause very few ripples in their business. But, if little DASA Corporation's one and only building burned to the ground, the company would be permanently closed the next day. Call me a pessimist. Fine. Read on.

So, I thought and thought and then thought some more. Then my rational side said: Ask yourself: What's the worst outcome even if the place burned to the ground? You're young. Your wife is young. Your son is young. You're all healthy. You'll have great new experience to add to your resume. Then you'll go out and find another job just like you did before when you were laid off by Kimberly-Clark. Then I said to myself: Self, you know, that makes perfect sense! If I'm going to take risks with my career and with my family's lives, now is the time when we can most easily absorb such risks. So I finally accepted the job as Personnel Director for DASA Corporation.

It was the dead of winter when I was to start work in Massachusetts. If you think that God doesn't have a strange sense of humor you are very mistaken.

I was to go ahead of Susan and Eric to get settled in Massachusetts. Because of a major snowstorm on the day of my flight to Boston, the flight was cancelled. Not a good start on this move. A bad omen? It gets better. I frantically booked a seat on a train from New York to Boston. Just getting to Grand Central Station from our apartment in Queens was a nightmare in itself, but I got there and boarded my train. What would normally be a three-hour trip took more than six hours due to snow drifts that had to be cleared from the tracks. The train stopped many times along the way. There was a blizzard roiling out there.

I knew that on the evening of my arrival there was going to be a dinner held for the company management team, and I was to be introduced to them at this dinner. Though it was out of my control, I worried greatly that I might not be able to make the dinner. The train finally arrived in Boston, and when I stepped outside the station all I could see were high walls of plowed snow. Thirty-five inches of snow had fallen! In New York City, three point five inches of snow would paralyze the city. But this was New England. Here they were prepared to deal with monster snowfalls, and much to my amazement, I was able to quickly find a taxi to Andover, about 35 miles north of Boston, and the roadways were amazingly clear, notwithstanding the huge walls of piled snow on the sides of the roads.

I finally arrived at the restaurant where they were waiting for me. Exhausted and disheveled, I took my seat with a group of total strangers (except for my mentor), wondering about all the bad omens that had already occurred in just my first long day of work, and not five minutes after I had sat down, someone came bursting through the doors into our banquet room screaming: *The plant's on fire!!*

My worst nightmare had just come true!

As it turned out, the fire, thank God (yes, the same God with the sick sense of humor), was extinguished by the sprinkler system with little damage to property and no damage to people or equipment. It soon became apparent that the fire had been intentionally set. The night security guard said that he discovered the fire and saw someone outside a nearby window who threw a brick at him through the closed window and then ran away. He had a bruise on his head from the brick but nothing serious.

There was only one aspect of the guard's story that clearly did not make sense. The broken glass from the window was all on the outside of the building. None was on the inside. How does a brick thrown from outside the window cause the broken window glass to be on the outside of the building? The guard was confronted by the police and ultimately confessed to deliberately setting the fire in a stack of scrap cardboard, directly, with intent, under a sprinkler head. His motive? He didn't want to burn down the building; he wanted attention as the hero that was wounded while chasing away an arsonist.

I went on from this epic first day on the job to work for DASA for five years. Did I get a great deal of valuable experience that I couldn't have gotten in the same amount of time if I'd remained with J. C. Penney? You bet. Did I have fun and meet some wonderful folks some of whom are still friends today? You bet. Was there a painful price for my family and me to pay for this experience? You bet.

DASA grew quickly and exponentially by adding products and through mergers, and the employee population mushroomed from a couple of hundred to over a thousand. These were exciting times. I was learning a lot and working very long hours. It was a reasonable tradeoff for me, my time in exchange for the experience. About halfway through my employment at DASA it became clear that the company was overextended and that the president of the company had personal, ulterior motives, which did not include any interest in the corporate good. Translation: He wanted to make a lot of money and didn't care about anyone but himself. He was a very bright and charismatic individual, but self-absorbed and had little integrity.

Chapter 19

Good Fortune Crumbles

As time went by DASA shifted into reverse gear. Where we'd grown through merger and acquisition, now we began divesting assets. As this regression continued the result was chaos, fear, and regular weekly layoffs of employees, and I was the executioner in charge of the layoff process. The handwriting was on the wall. The company was not likely to survive. I needed to start looking for another job. My former mentor left DASA, making me feel much more vulnerable. It was 1973 and there was a recession going on. Not the ideal time to be looking for a job.

It was during this turbulent time in my career that I became a greatly troubled person. I was depressed, angry, and filled with fear. I spoke with my doctor who advised me to begin taking Valium, which I was very reluctant to do. He convinced me by asking: If you had a headache would you take aspirin? I said, yes. Then he said, well, if you're having emotional pain, take Valium. I accepted his advice and analogy and began to take Valium. It was very helpful in alleviating my symptoms. However, there was less public information at the time about the powerful addictive nature of Valium and how its effect is dangerously compounded by taking it along with alcohol.

I took 10 mg of Valium the moment I opened my eyes in the morning, and another dose every few hours until I was taking 60 mg a day—a large amount. Susan and I got into the habit of going out every Friday night with DASA friends to unwind at a nearby hotel lounge where I would drink myself blind, almost literally. After several martinis along with my evening dose of Valium, I would drive home late in the evening with severe tunnel vision, against Susan's pleas to let her drive. I'd awake the next day remembering little if anything about the previous night. It wasn't until years later that I discovered how much danger I was in when combining my high consumption of Valium with alcohol. Many people died by doing exactly what I was doing as Valium became the most abused prescription drug in the country.

After being on Valium for years at the time we moved to St. Louis, Missouri, I saw a new doctor and told him about my medical history and my Valium addiction. He said simply: Stop taking it. Being the classic accommodating and trusting patient that I was, I stopped taking Valium, cold turkey. This did not work out too well. Within a couple of days I began having severe withdrawal symptoms. Headaches, muscle tremors, heavy perspiration; in general, the feelings that you get with a severe case of flu. I was afraid to tell my boss what was happening out of fear of the impact on my career; my boss was a very straight-laced person. So I would drag myself to work every day, doing the best that I could to hide my symptoms, enduring until the time that I could go home and crash into bed. This severe withdrawal trauma continued for a week without let up. I was at a breaking point. I called my doctor and he explained that what I was experiencing was not unusual considering my history, and that the symptoms might continue for another week or more. I could not imagine surviving another week of torment while trying to do my job as though all was well. My emotional and physical strength were just too close to the edge of exhaustion.

The doctor said that what I could do to make the withdrawal more tolerable is to begin taking half doses every day for a week or two, then taper off to half doses every other day, and so forth, until I felt able to stop completely. I remember vividly that when I hung up the phone after the conversation with my doctor and took a half dose of Valium, that I felt better almost immediately. I followed this withdrawal treatment plan and after a few weeks I remember leaving the house for work in the morning having not taken any Valium, but having one pill tucked in my pocket just in case. I felt proud of what I'd accomplished, but it was one year before I felt comfortable enough leaving the house without a Valium in my pocket.

Life lesson: Addiction can occur easier than you think, and trying to shake addictions can be infinitely more difficult than you can imagine, because the addiction is both physical and psychological. The physical part is much easier to conquer, hence the psychologically needed pill-in-my-pocket every day for a year.

Chapter 20

Goodbye DASA

I began circulating my resumé but opportunities were very limited because of the recession. My former DASA mentor was now a VP for HR at a large department store corporation, The May Department Stores Company. On his recommendation I eventually accepted a job with a May Company Division called Venture Stores, the only discount store division in the corporation, based in St. Louis, Missouri. The same man who started Target Stores for the Dayton Hudson Company, John Geiss, was hired by the May Company to create Venture Stores to be similar to Target. The "one stop shopping" concept—general merchandise, groceries, auto service, pharmacy, and a food court, all under one roof—now so common—was a new idea at the time and a very successful idea indeed.

And so the Duchin family, now including three children—Eric 7, Andrea 3, and Adam 1—moved to St. Louis, and I began my job as Director of Training & Development for this growing and successful business with stores in Missouri, Illinois, and Kansas, with new stores opening regularly. I progressed steadily from my initial position, to

Director of Organization Development, then to Divisional Vice President, and then to a full VP position. I was thoroughly immersed in my work and loving it.

Here again my work weeks were long but I was gaining more experience and regular promotions. After 10 years at Venture Stores I felt that I'd earned the privilege of being considered for a Sr. HR VP position at one of the May Company divisions. These were the top positions in HR at The May Company other than positions at the corporate office in downtown St. Louis, but I wanted to be where the action was, in the stores. Eventually there was an opening for a Sr. HR VP at the May Company department store division, Meier & Frank, in Portland, Oregon. It was offered to me and I accepted. You know the saying "be careful what you wish for?" I was about to learn the hard way how true this could be.

We moved to Portland in 1984. My wonderful and accommodating wife continued to fully support my career decisions, but our children were not at all happy about the move. At least not the two younger children. Our son Eric was at the time a freshman at the University of Missouri, and he was not planning to move with us. Andrea was about to enter high school, and Adam was in junior high. Our children had grown up in St. Louis, where we lived for 12 years. They'd made many good friends, and Portland is a long way from St. Louis. Nonetheless, I rationalized that what I was doing was for the common good of our family, and we began a new life once again in another new place.

Soon after, it struck me that for many years now I'd been rationalizing my decisions, and that in truth I was placing my desires above the collective good of my family. I regretted this unavoidable fact for many years after . . . still do to some extent.

Let's rewind the timeframe a bit. When I'd been with Venture Stores in St. Louis for around two years, a young man who had been working for Venture Stores in the Kansas City area, and who had little if any HR experience, was hired by my boss, the Sr. VP of HR, to fill an open position working for me, and this happened without my foreknowledge while I was on vacation. I was furious that my boss would do something like this. I felt undermined and I told him so. The young man hired by my boss was Ron Lucas, and his wife's name is Karen.

Notwithstanding the inauspicious start to our working relationship I immediately liked Ron, and within a short time, we became friends. In the years to come, Ron and Karen became Susan's and my best friends. And, Ron and Karen were the vessels used by God to introduce us to Jesus Christ as our personal Lord and Savior. In large part this happened through the Lucas' third child, their only son, David. The Lucas' had two daughters before David's birth.

Ron was tall, physically strong, unassuming, with boyish good looks. I always hoped that Ron would have the blessing of a son so that he could connect on a man-to-man level with a male child.

Karen was a lovely woman, with a flashing smile and eyes that seemed to look into you as well as at you. There were no airs about her, or Ron for that matter, and Susan and I liked them immediately.

David Lucas, however, was born severely handicapped. He was blind and deaf, could only be fed with a tube inserted into his throat, could make sounds but never spoke, and never walked. It was a heartbreaking reality, to say the least.

Yet, Susan and I never heard a single complaint from Ron or Karen, and they always seemed to be at peace with their burden. It was troubling and puzzling to me. How could parents with such a burden possess such peace in their hearts when confronted 24/7 with the continuous and special care that David's conditions demanded?

Karen, in a recent phone conversation that she and I had, reminded me of an incident that I'd forgotten. She said that she and Ron were talking about this recently. I'd walked into Ron's office at work one day, closed the door behind me, looked at Ron and said: "How do you do it?" He understood the context of my question and replied with one word: "Jesus." Not at all satisfied with his response I turned and walked out.

Susan and I grew to love Ron and Karen and their children, and we had a special heart for David. Parents with special needs children need a break once in a while, but I don't recall that there were any friends willing to care for David so that Ron and Karen could get some relief—except Susan and me, especially Susan. The scariest part was the tube feeding, as well as the prospect of what would be the outcome if David became injured or seriously ill, or even worse, if he died while in our care? We accepted the risks and took David into our care temporarily every so often. We did it because we loved our friends and they needed the assistance. It was humbling and uncomfortable taking responsibility for David even for just a day or two, but it gave us a vividly clarified understanding of what Ron and Karen were faced with every minute of every day.

David was not expected to live long. He died at the age of 11. It was the firm and unequivocal faith in Jesus Christ displayed by Ron and Karen Lucas, through their surrender to Him as they loved and cared for their dear son David, that drew me to want to know more about this Jewish guy, Jesus.

After years of close friendship with the Lucas', one Christmas, having had many conversations with them over time about faith, and after many, many questions that I threw at them, Karen gave me a Bible and said: "All the answers to your questions are in here." You know something? She was spot on!

I began to read the Bible every morning before going to work, starting on page one of Genesis, the first book of the Bible. Where else do you start a book, in the middle? As I read God's words recorded by his chosen spokespersons, I drew closer and closer to Him. It was very exciting to see each morning what God was going to reveal.

When I reached the book of the prophet Isaiah, and read chapter 53, God spoke dramatically and firmly to my heart and to my spirit that the suffering servant vividly described in this chapter was His Son, Jesus. Further, God said to me that I now had a choice to make. I could believe it and accept Jesus as the promised Messiah, or not. This is the ultimate dilemma of Free Will. I was truly terrified that I'd "heard" and "felt" God's voice. I thought that my heart would explode out of my chest. It was extraordinary, exciting, and frightening.

I continued to read my Bible every morning, now expecting that I would hear God's voice each time I opened His book. Within a short time I reached the New Testament book of Romans, chapter 10, verse

9, where it states: "that if you confess with your mouth Jesus as Lord, and believe in your heart that God raised Him from the dead, you shall be saved." When I read this verse my spirit immediately connected it to what God revealed to me while reading Isaiah 53. At that very moment I was so powerfully convicted in my heart of the truth presented to me, and of the evident continuity of the Old and the New Testaments, that I truly believed that if I did not confess and accept Jesus at that very moment, that my pounding heart would cease beating and I would die. With a reverent fear, and a firm conviction of truth that I was blessed to receive in a wonderful way, I confessed Jesus as Lord and accepted Him as my Messiah right then and there, while all alone in my bedroom.

Of course I shared my experience with Susan whom I'd been pestering with Bible verses now for months. She was excited for me but clearly not on the same page. When I shared my newfound faith with Ron and Karen Lucas they just smiled and said that they could see it on my face before I said a word, and told me that they had been praying for Susan and me for a long time. We now not only had best friends, we had a new brother and sister. Susan and Karen became very close. Karen told me during our recent conversation that she's never had a friend as dear to her as Susan. I know that Susan felt the same way about Karen.

Don't worry, I'm not going to launch into a sermon here calling for you to give your life to Jesus. Though that's not the worst thing you could do. I will say that my new faith gave me different eyes through which the world around me now took on different hues and casts than before. This didn't happen with a flash of lightning or a cloud of smoke, it just evolved. As I studied God's word, His Bible, that I like to refer to as "The Manufacturer's Handbook," I learned more about how God expects me to live out my life. As I grew in my faith, I still had on the top of my list to attain a Sr. VP position with the May Company. I even regularly prayed for this.

Susan and Karen Lucas were very closely knit together in friendship. As Karen told me recently, she'd commented to Susan that it was no fun to clean her house alone. So, Susan suggested that they help each other have more 'fun' cleaning their homes by doing it together. They'd both clean one of their houses, and when finished, would together clean the other's house. They had a wonderful time together talking about life as they stood together in the shower stall scrubbing the tiles.

Karen reminded me that she and Susan were in a bowling league together. Karen said that Susan was the best bowler on their team, and that she was the worst. Susan always encouraged Karen and every year that their team participation continued, Karen won the trophy for the most improved bowler.

Karen said that Susan had the biggest heart for service to others than anyone she's ever known. No argument here!

Chapter 21

Escaping The Frying Pan

Remember a while back I stated: "Be careful what you wish for?". Well, I got my wish, and the result was clearly not what I expected.

Now, at Meier & Frank in Portland, Oregon, I was the Sr. VP for HR for a $220 million dollar company, with thousands of employees, and my own HR staff of 23 people. I'd reached the career pinnacle I so wanted to reach. It very soon became hell on earth. Why? From a human perspective the other senior officers, including the president, and the chairman, were driven by one thing: money. The more profit the company made the more money they would get in bonuses and stock options. Employees? Well, people were secondary considerations at best. Remember, I was the Sr. VP for Human Resources. My 'business' was the people of the company. My role, and my philosophy of how to do my job, was to walk a tightrope between helping to meet the financial goals of the company, and seeking the wellbeing of the company's employees. With a president and chairman as driven by money as they were, we were bound to clash often. And we did.

Overlay the fact that I was now trying to live my life in accordance with Biblical principles, and it became quickly evident that I could not serve God with honor in that environment. My dreams appeared to be collapsing on top of me. I'd gotten to where I wanted to be in my career, I got what I'd asked God to give me, and I was miserable. I would go home after a 12 hour work day and sit on the floor in our bedroom with Susan and cry. We prayed together, and for the first time in my life I prayed for God to put me wherever He wanted me to be, but to please get me out of my current job. It was killing me spiritually and I believe physically as well. It wasn't doing my family any good either.

I began to circulate my resumé and talk with friends about my dilemma. It had occurred to me (and I hoped it was God putting the idea in my head) that any other large retail organization would likely be fraught with the same issues. Though I had considerable experience in the retail world, I was convinced that my HR skills were transferable. After all, people are people. Therefore, the kinds of people issues that arise are the same regardless of the industry.

Susan and I invited our pastor and his wife, Randy and Diane Roth, over for dinner and I shared with them that I was invited to interview for a job at a small college in California. I'd never heard of the school and had never been to California. I asked them if they might know anything about the college because it was a Christian school. They asked the name of the school, and I told them it was Westmont College in Santa Barbara, California. They looked at each other and laughed. I asked them what was so funny? Randy replied: We both graduated from Westmont College. Go interview and take the job!

Amazing how God works in our lives when we yield to His love and His power to do anything.

Chapter 22

Off to California

In 1986 I accepted the job as Director of Human Resources at Westmont College in Santa Barbara, California, leaving my position as Sr. VP at Meier & Frank in Portland, Oregon. Westmont is a small Christian college with 1200 students, on a gorgeous 135 acre campus in the heart of Montecito, California, the location of many exclusive estates and home to many celebrities. Think Oprah.

This move resonated well with the whole family. A good omen for a change.

I gave up a six figure salary with stock options, a company car, yadda, yadda, yadda, and accepted a two-thirds cut in pay, to move to a place and a job where I hoped that I could serve God openly and effectively.

It took eight months to sell our beautiful, new, custom-built 2600 square foot English Tudor home in Portland. We received one offer during this eight months and took a loss on the sale.

I had been working at Westmont College during this long transition for our family, living rent-free in a cottage on the college's campus, with the free use of a car owned by the college. Susan would travel down from Portland every few weeks to join me in house hunting. After finally selling our home in Portland, I found a 1600 square foot home in Goleta, California, 20 minutes west of Santa Barbara, without Susan ever seeing the house before her arriving to move in with our family! The reason for this was that properties were selling so quickly in the Santa Barbara market that there was not enough time for Susan to rush down in a day or so to look at the house before making an offer. Though I was very uncomfortable with this situation, she and our children loved the house and we moved in during the summer of 1986. The house was in turnkey condition, and all our furniture from the much larger Portland house fit well, albeit less spread out. Everything fell into place, this time in accordance with God's timing, not mine. I was very satisfied with this arrangement.

I spent the next 20 years as Director of HR at Westmont College before retiring in July 2006. I could go on and on about how different working at a not-for-profit college is compared with a for-profit corporation. Suffice to say that I learned a lot about the world of higher education, had a wonderful boss who became a good friend, worked with many wonderful people, and some not-so-wonderful people (hey, we're still on this side of Heaven, right?), no longer needed to work 60 hour weeks, never worked on weekends, valued the way faith was integrated into teaching at this excellent Christian college of the liberal arts and sciences, and was blessed that two of my children were able to attend and graduate Westmont College because of the deeply discounted high tuition that was a unique employee benefit.

Chapter 23

Blunders and Blessings

Life Lesson: This one is a biggie.

As I look over my shoulder at the life I've led until now, based on most peoples' standards, I feel that I've led a decent life. Undoubtedly, my parents would have said so; they were very proud of my career successes, loved Susan as their own daughter, and adored their grandchildren. I've been faithful to my wife, and earned a very good living for my family.

However, most peoples' standards don't necessarily equate to what's right or best. I missed the mark in very important areas, and I still regret these big misses.

I put my career ahead of my family for over 20 years. This was an enormous mistake driven by aspirations commonly held by many people: success in your job equals success in your family life. This is so off base that its pathetic. With blunt simplicity Jesus told His disciples that you can't serve two masters. Either you will love the one and hate the other, or vice versa. This is so true and cuts so deeply, as truth often does.

I put my craving for success, which became my master, above my love for my family. For this I am deeply ashamed. The result was that not only did I drag my family after me each time I took a new job in a new place to further advance my career, without caring enough about how these changes disrupted their lives, it also resulted in my not spending enough precious time with my wife and children because of the long hours that I worked and how emotionally drained I was when I was at home.

Thank God that Susan had a clear and correct compass bearing on life goals and values. She wanted to be a full-time, stay-at-home mom, so that she could be an anchor for our children, to be there when they came home from school every afternoon, and to be able to nurture and teach them important life values, typically by personal example. She did this with great skill, wisdom, tenderness, great patience, unconditional love, and great joy, all of which came naturally to her. Remember one of the questions I pondered when I was thinking of asking Susan to marry me? It was: Did I believe that she would be a good mother to our children? Susan hit a grand slam on this one!

One of the memories of something that I did do right is that I was home for dinner with the family just about every night. Often, dinner was late because I got home late, but thankfully my family waited for me. This was a very special and important time of connecting with each other and talking about the day's happenings; the kids' day in school, what they did that day with their friends, issues they were dealing with. Sounds like simple stuff, doesn't it? I'll tell you this. Years later, when our children were grown, they told us how important our dinner times together were to them. They reminded us how friends of theirs who were often guests at our table for meals were so surprised and delighted at how open our table conversation was and that their parents would never discuss with them the kinds of topics that were fair game at our mealtimes.

When I found myself simultaneously at the pinnacle of my career I was also in the darkest valley of misery. Abandoning the high pay, high demand job as a Sr. Vice President, and taking an enormous reduction in pay in a new job, was a welcome and prayed-for escape for me. It also was a dramatic life lesson being played out in real time, in particular for my children.

Here was their dad, a high-powered executive, making a lot of money, turning his back on a lucrative lifestyle, taking a much smaller job, and accepting an enormous cut in pay and benefits, in order to live a more reasonable life, have more time with his family, and to have an opportunity to use his skills to help a Christian ministry.

It is my belief that this change that I made in my life may have positively influenced my children's planning of their own lives. First, to follow their hearts, rather than to seek the best paying opportunities. And second, to put their family's best interests above all else.

Perhaps my children are just smarter than I was from the get go. To wit: our oldest child, Eric, enlisted in the U.S.A.F. and made it his career for 24 years, rising to the rank of Master Sergeant, and serving honorably including being part of the first U.S. military presence on the ground in Saudi Arabia, with the F-15s of the 1st Tactical Fighter Squadron, during the first Gulf War.

Our daughter, Andrea, after graduating Westmont College with a B.A. in Sociology, got her M.A. in Social Work from the Heller School at Brandeis University, intending to work in her field as an administrator. After marrying a man with four children from a previous marriage, and then having her own children, she became a dedicated stay-at-home mom, just like her mom.

Our younger son, Adam, graduated Westmont with a B.A. in Religious Studies, went on to get his Masters of Theology from Talbot Seminary, and serves as a pastor specializing in worship arts and youth ministry.

None of these careers will likely make my children wealthy, at least not in the eyes of many people in the world around us. They followed their hearts, and so were a giant step ahead of me compared with when I was making career and family choices at their ages. Whatever their reasons for the decisions they made, I am grateful to see the results of their choices, and very proud of each of them. Susan would say, Amen!

Chapter 24

Terrible Loneliness

On February 27, 2011, two days after her 68th birthday, when she was too weak to even open the birthday card that I brought to her bedside in the hospital ICU, the love of my life, my sweet, sweet, Susan, the dearest person I've ever known, died right in front of my eyes.

During our lives together, living without Susan was unimaginable, and even though this is now my reality, its still unimaginable. I know that this makes no sense, but it is what I'm often feeling.

On some days I'll wake at three in the morning believing that Susan is with me. I hear her moving about, and sometimes for a brief moment I see her in the shadows. These occurrences disturb me so much that I felt the need to turn the bedside lamp on if I was to have any hope of getting back to sleep. This was the most dramatic of many similar events that have happened to me, especially in the middle of the night. Now, I don't feel the need for the bedside lamp to be on, but I keep a lamp on in the front hallway to dispel shadows. Silly, huh? Grief plays many nasty tricks on the mind.

Susan and I never spoke about how it might be for the survivor after one of us died. It wasn't that we were afraid to talk about it, it just wasn't something that seemed real to us. Even when we had a will and a family trust created, it just seemed like a sensible step to take. It never caused us any angst.

The loneliness now is simply terrible.

> Samuel Johnson, an English poet and author in the 18th century, summed it up very well following the death of his wife:
>
> *"I have ever since seemed to myself broken off from mankind; a kind of solitary wanderer in the wild of life, without any direction, or fixed point of view: a gloomy gazer on the world to which I have little relation."*

> Charles Dickens posed this remarkable and poignant question:
>
> *"And can it be that in a world so full and busy, the loss of one weak creature makes a void in any heart, so wide and deep that nothing but the width and depth of vast eternity can fill it up?"*

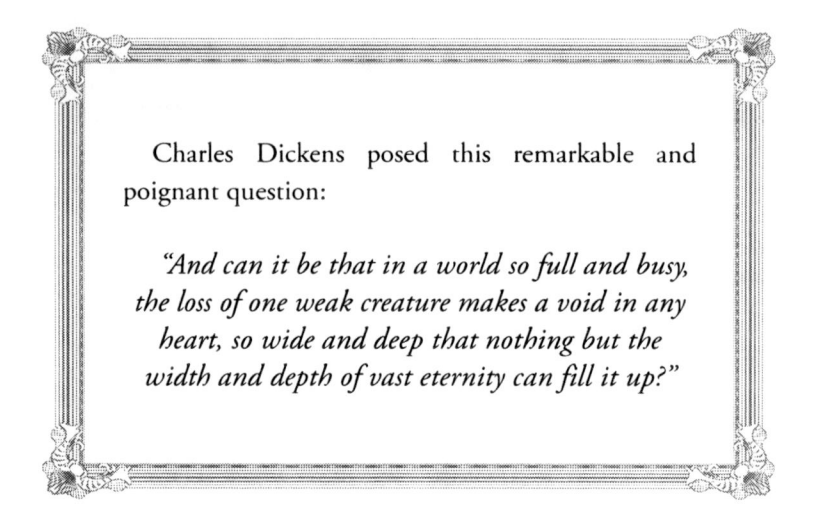

My response to Dickens question is, most assuredly, yes. And, if a person can answer "yes" to this question, that person has had the rare good fortune to know someone in a way that many never have and perhaps never will.

So, as irrational as it may seem to some, I consider myself extraordinarily fortunate to have a deep void in my heart because of the great loss that I've suffered: the loss of the love of my life. We were married for 47 years, and knew each other for 54 years. You might say that we had a lifetime together. I would say that I've not had enough of her.

Chapter 25

The First 22 Days

I sent the following letter to friends and relatives early in my grieving for Susan, just a few weeks after she died. I needed to try to drain some of the constant pain I was feeling.

- - - - - - - - - - - -

You have been so wonderfully caring and kind to me at this difficult time in my life. Your fellowship, calls, food, and prayers, nourish my body, spirit and soul. I thank you with all my heart.

I find that putting my feelings in writing is helpful to my journey toward healing following the tragic and sudden passing of my beloved wife, Susan. I share my writings with you because you are dear friends and relatives and in this way I can 'talk' to all of you at the same time.

I hope that it does not trouble you to look through this window onto my passage through grieving. I welcome you looking through my window and beg your continued prayers for this hard journey that I'm on.

It has been 22 days and the tears keep coming each day. At first I worried that I would not or could not cry. There is no longer any such absurd thought in mind. Sometimes the tears are blindingly profuse. And with the tears comes physical pain and fear; a tightness in my chest as well as uncontrollable shaking of my hands. The tears seem to drain my energy, like a seizure of my soul.

Yet I believe that I have found reason to be thankful for my tears. While reading a book about grieving the following thoughts came to mind.

Susan and I became one when we married 47 years ago. This was an emotional and spiritual connecting of the two of us. But there was another dimension, perhaps the most important but the least understood: We became one flesh in the eyes of God. The way God performs this miracle is so perfect and wondrously beyond our comprehension, that there is no physical manifestation of it. But it does happen.

How can I be so sure of something that might be so inconceivable or controversial to many people? Because the proof of it comes to bear with excruciating reality when one partner is lost.

When one-half of this miraculous, humanly incomprehensible uniting of husband and wife departs, the disunion is like a surgical separation of two hearts, minds, and spirits, that have lived in a marvelous, invisible dimension that we are not conscious of on a day-to-day basis.

The separation, unlike the union, has a terrible conscious aspect, like surgery without anesthesia ... unspeakable pain and anguish. How might it feel to suddenly lose one of your limbs with no medical assistance for the shock and pain? Thus, how would I expect that suddenly losing one half of my being would not be immeasurably more terrible.

As I cried today, I believe that God impressed upon me that my tears are not just a necessary and unavoidable part of the physical and emotional grieving process, but that my tears were like fluid that must drain from a physical wound in order for the wound to properly heal.

The wound is the horrendous tearing apart that has recently occurred. And if my tears are part of the healing of this wound, then I welcome the tears, and thank God for imparting to me tender insight just when I need it the most.

Susan passed on so suddenly that we did not have the chance to say goodbye to one another. This is excruciatingly sad for me. However, we had gotten into the habit in the past few years of saying to each other, every day: "I love you today." I am so grateful that this daily habit can in some small way substitute for a final goodbye that I'm not even sure that I could have brought myself to say anyway.

My dear ones, each one of us and those we love are all just one breath away from the physical ties to each other and to this Earth. If you have a loved one that you have not told that you love them today, or as often as you possibly can, even if it's not wholehearted each time, I exhort you to do so. The blessing of it is that the more you say it the more you feel it. And if a sudden loss of a loved one occurs for you as it did for me, you will find comfort in knowing that you so recently expressed your love for the person lost.

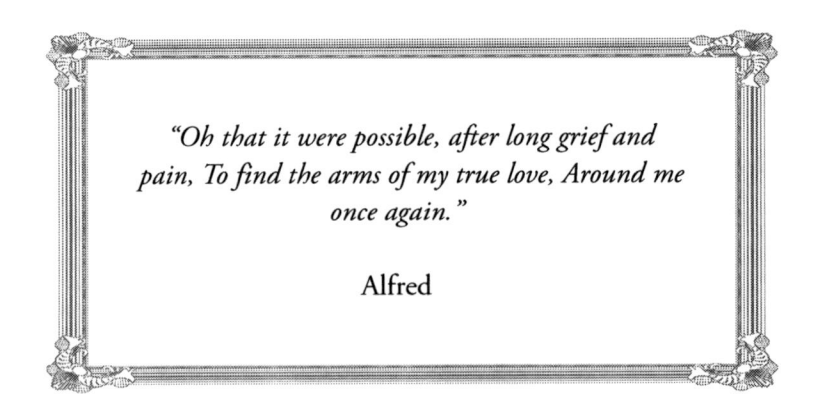

> "Oh that it were possible, after long grief and pain, To find the arms of my true love, Around me once again."
>
> Alfred

Chapter 26

Life Forever Changed

After being at Susan's side in her hospital room through an interminably long and terrifying night, I stared at Susan's face at 10:45 am, as her shallow breathing suddenly stopped. My heart rate suddenly surged, and I became lightheaded. This was what the doctor said would be the sign that she would soon be gone. An eternal 10 seconds later, as I watched in helpless horror, she finally took a breath, and then again, no breathing for 20 seconds. Then another breath, followed by no more breathing. I screamed for my son Adam, who was with me on this fateful morning, to run and get a nurse. But I knew that Susan was gone.

It was only 36 hours earlier that Susan's Oncologist told me the grim news that her cancer had spread too rapidly for any medical interventions, and, if that wasn't shocking enough, he said that she might have only hours left. Hours!

I left the hospital that evening to go home to try to get some sleep, and when I returned to the hospital early the next morning, Susan was unresponsive. About 27 hours later she died having never regained consciousness.

My life had cruelly and forever been changed in just a few hours, after 47 years of marriage to the sweetest, kindest, most forgiving and loving person I've ever known: My dear, dear, wife, Susan. Oh how I love and miss her!

Now I grieve my terrible loss trying to move forward toward God only knows what. I live on memories both sweet and bitter. All these memories are part of who we were together, and so they are precious to me because it's all I now have of her. Remembered stories, photographs, conversations, places we lived, our children, grandchildren, friends and neighbors, favorite foods she cooked, vacation spots, our intimacy that we shared for so long, and letters we wrote to each other when we were teenagers; 85 letters that Susan saved and had safely tucked away that I recently rediscovered.

These letters are among the most wonderful treasures that I possess. Someday I will pass them down to my children so that they might have an intimate glimpse of how their mother's and father's love for one another began and grew. Some of these letters are shared in this book.

Chapter 27

Triggers

I recently heard the following classic oldie on the radio and I was touched deeply as I could not help but relate its simple lyrics to my love for Susan. It brought tears to my eyes once again.

ARTIST: "Firefall"
TITLE: *"You Are the Woman"*

You are the woman that I've always dreamed of
I knew it from the start
I saw your face and that's the last I've seen of my heart

It's not so much the things you say to me
It's not the things you do
It's how I feel each time you're close to me
That keeps me close to you

You are the woman that I've always dreamed of
I knew it from the start
I saw your face and that's the last I've seen of my heart

It's not so much your pretty face I see
It's not the clothes you wear
It's more that special way you look at me
That always keeps me there

You are the woman that I've always dreamed of
I knew it from the start
I saw your face and that's the last I've seen of my heart

It's hard to tell you all the love I'm feelin'
That's just not my style
You got a way to set my senses reelin'
Every time you smile

You are the woman that I've always dreamed of
I knew it from the start
I saw your face and that's the last I've seen of my heart

> *"Life's greatest happiness is to be convinced we are loved."*
>
> Victor Hugo, *Les Miserables*

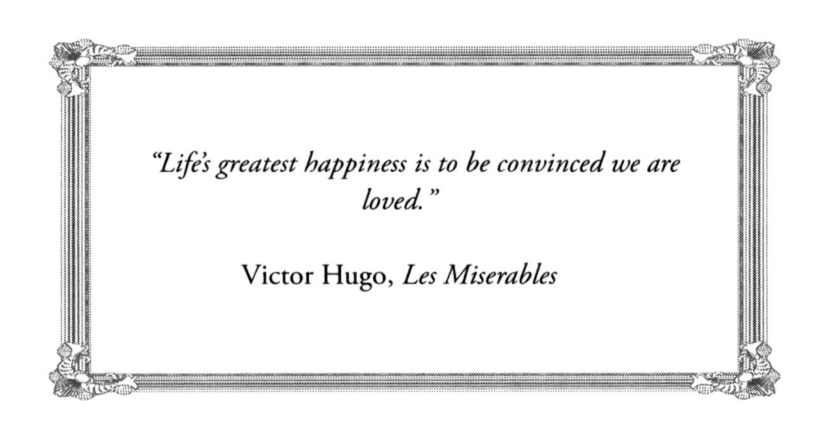

Chapter 28

The Great Fall, or, . . .
The Great Performance?

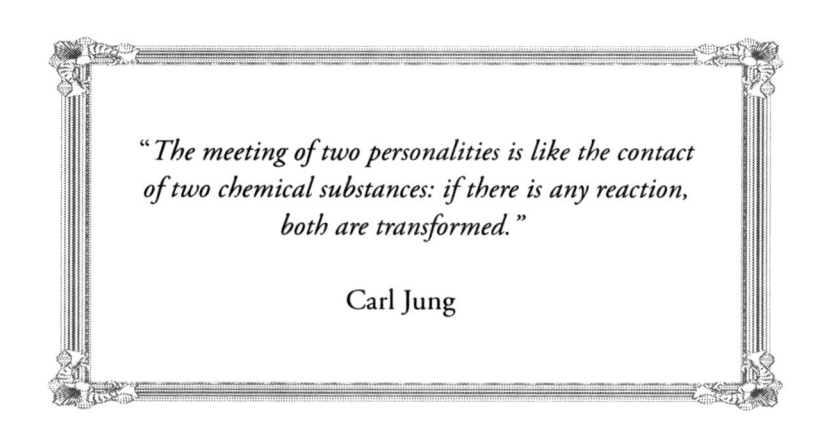

> *"The meeting of two personalities is like the contact of two chemical substances: if there is any reaction, both are transformed."*
>
> Carl Jung

It all began for Susan and me during the summer of 1957, at a small resort hotel not unlike the backdrop of the movie "Dirty Dancing." (If you've never seen this classic film starring Patrick Swayze and Jennifer Gray, you should: Great 1960s music, great dancing, great story, happy ending.)

Splat! Quick as a wink she's lying on the ground shaken some by her awkward tumble. This is cute and funny when a six year old gets more or less harmlessly tossed from the low-to-the-ground, little self-propelled merry-go-round. No motor driven contraptions in this 1950s day camp play area. The merry-go-round was set in motion by gripping the round, iron braces set upright from its shiny aluminum surface, pushing and running alongside it, and then jumping on and hanging on to fight the centrifugal force, until it slowed and eventually stopped, or threw you off in a fairly benign way. Kids often jumped off while it was spinning just for the heck of it.

Susan, however, the girl now sprawled on the ground in front of me, was not six years old. She was a very cute and precocious 14 year old girl on the cusp of womanhood who was hanging around trying to get my attention. I was 16 years old, working part-time helping with the kids at the day camp at this small, summer resort, the Manhattan Hotel. This very modest hotel was in the sleepy, little country town of Ellenville, New York, in the heart of the Catskill Mountains, 100 miles north of the Bronx, New York. Our respective parents, who had never met before, just happened to choose to spend some vacation time this July at the same vacation spot, temporarily escaping from the hot and muggy Bronx, where both families lived the other 50 weeks of the year.

Now sitting in the well-worn dusty dirt track that circled the merry-go-round, Susan looked very inelegant, and very embarrassed. I moved quickly to help her to her feet and to see if anything other than her pride was injured. I remember this clearly with a broad smile even now. She was very embarrassed, or, she seemed to be. Yet, I wonder if it was all an act to get my attention. Either way, it was our first face-to-face connection, albeit very brief. I guess the "accident" worked.

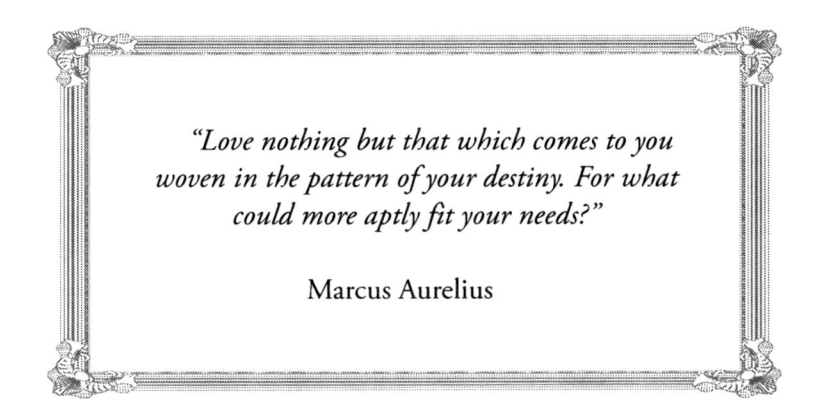

> "Love nothing but that which comes to you woven in the pattern of your destiny. For what could more aptly fit your needs?"
>
> Marcus Aurelius

Chapter 29

Summer of 1957

Summer vacations out of the city were a luxury for middle-class New Yorkers, and my family's vacations in the country, which didn't happen every year, typically lasted for a couple of weeks. During this time my father continued to work in the city Mondays through part of Fridays, and then he would make the three hour drive on Fridays to be with us until he left very early the following Monday morning to return to work in the city.

Yeah, I know. You're doing the math and wondering why it would take three hours to drive 100 miles. Remember: 1957? There were no superhighways, thus speed limits were lower than they are today. Then there was usually the crush of traffic leaving the city for points north on weekends during the summer. And if you were unlucky enough to get behind an 18-wheeler on some of the single lane roads . . . fuhgeddaboudit!

Susan's family vacation at the Manhattan Hotel ended before mine, and so they left for home before my family did. I remained at the hotel for the rest of the summer, working, after my parents left for home.

My father had a first cousin, Merty Duchin, who lived with his wife, Naomi, and four daughters, in Liberty, N.Y., not far from the Manhattan Hotel. Merty was a partner in a very successful insurance agency that insured many of the resorts in the area including some of the most famous resorts in the country at that time, like The Concord Hotel, which could seat a thousand people in its entertainment center. This was the heyday for the Catskill Mountains resort area which boomed with thousands of vacationers between Memorial Day and Labor Day each summer. The Manhattan Hotel was one of cousin Merty's accounts and he recommended it to my family. It fit our budget.

Merty and his lovely and unbelievably energetic wife, Naomi, had a beautiful home. I always thought it was ironic that Merty didn't have a son because Merty was a man's man; robust, strong, broad-chested, thick wavy hair, and a disarming, broad, warm smile. He should have had at least one son. This worked to my advantage because he treated me like a son and I often visited their home, hanging out with the oldest daughter, my cousin Joyce, who was my age.

When I visited their home I slept in a tight space in the attic, which, even though very hot in the summertime, was a special adventure for a kid from a small apartment in the Bronx. One of my fondest memories is that whenever my family vacationed in the Catskills, which usually was in July, cousin Naomi would deliver to me a homemade cake for my birthday, and man could she bake!

Back to the summer of 1957.

There is little detail that I now remember about my interactions with Susan after the fateful merry-go-round caper, and the formal introduction by her father, who I think was recruited by Susan to introduce us because I was very shy.

The Manhattan Hotel had a two-story main building where guests registered, and there was a small, dark, but cozy, lobby. It kind of resembled the Bates Motel house in the movie "Psycho". There were guest rooms on the second floor, probably a dozen or so. The rest of the hotel accommodations were u-shaped, connected, single story cottages that were larger than the rooms in the main house, more appropriate for families. We stayed in one of these cottages which had two bedrooms, and a bathroom that we shared with another family who occupied the other half of the suite. We always shared the cottage with good friends who lived near us in the Bronx, so it was a comfortable and enjoyable arrangement.

The hotel had what was called a "casino" on the premises, but not what jumps to mind when you think casino-equals-gambling. It was a simple, freestanding, single story building with an open floor plan and a stage where weekend entertainment took place. Often on weekends a professional comedian would be hired to perform. A band was on the hotel staff for the summer. They were usually young guys who played nightly and bunked in two small rooms on either side of the casino stage. Though they didn't get paid much, they had the easiest jobs of the hotel staff. They worked a few hours each night and had all day off to lounge around the pool and flirt with the girls.

I remember two girls, a year or two older than me, who were staying at the hotel with their families, who soon became well known for their escapades. One was named Fran, and I can't remember the other's name. Because of the small size of the hotel, and the clique that formed between most of the kids my age, including the guys in the band, there were no secrets, especially if the opportunity arose for guys to brag about conquests. In the short few weeks that Fran & friend were at the hotel, they'd gained a reputation for making out with lots of guys, letting the guys get their hands in their pants, and doing the same in return. This was amazingly exciting to me because I was as virgin as the first snowflake of winter and lived an exciting sex life through my buddies who were lucky enough to have their turns with these generous girls, and who liked to share their stories. But, kissing and hand jobs was as far as these teenage temptresses would go. After all, they wouldn't want to be known as sluts, would they?

I saw Susan and her family often at the casino in the evenings and at the pool during the day. Susan loved to dance and she was frequently on the dance floor in the evenings, especially doing the Lindy. I did not like to dance, but enjoyed watching others, especially women. To me, dancing was a socially acceptable release of sexual inhibitions. When women danced, their body movements were in themselves a form of secret pleasure for me, especially when dancing to sensuous Latin rhythms; Cha Cha, Merengue, Rhumba, which were the rage at the time.

During the day, when I wasn't working at the day camp, if I wasn't at the pool, I was hunting with my Red Ryder BB gun. I spent hours in the woods at the back of the hotel property honing my hunting skills. I think I single-handedly decimated the bird population in those woods, possibly creating some endangered species. Why did I enjoy the violence of shooting innocent birds? Though it was likely stored deep in my subconscious at the time, during adulthood I came to realize that it was anger towards my father. More to be told.

Though I didn't spend much time with Susan during our brief summer connection, something definitely clicked between us because I began to write letters to her from the Manhattan Hotel. I never imagined that this would be the beginning of an exchange of 85 letters before we were husband and wife, and the sowing of the first seeds of an extraordinary love that would grow between us.

For the moment, here were two teenagers, innocent in every sense of the word, who began to feel something for each other that they could not have articulated if their lives depended on it. It was the first tiny spark that lit a bit of kindling in our hearts, that slowly grew. Infant flames that were fanned into a delightful, mutual, roaring heart-fire, that burned for a very long time.

And so the seemingly random fickleness of time and place brought Susan Geller and Bob Duchin into each other's lives. Neither of us had the slightest inkling at the time of what life had in store for us down the road.

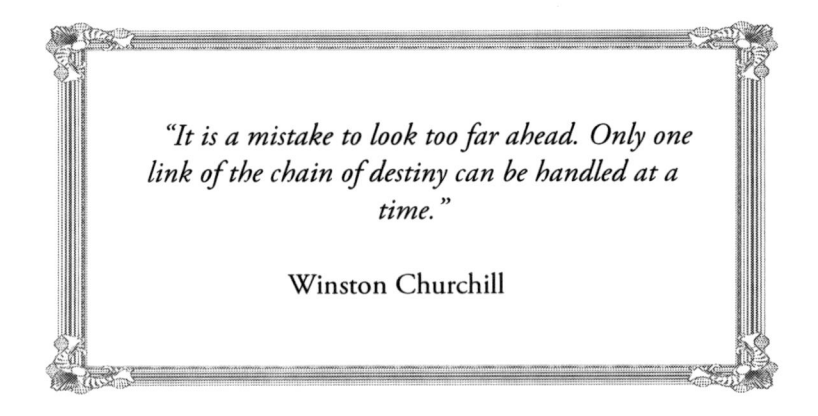

> *"It is a mistake to look too far ahead. Only one link of the chain of destiny can be handled at a time."*
>
> Winston Churchill

Chapter 30

First of 85 Love Letters

Though completely void of the kind of explicit passion that love letters might be expected to contain, in fact, void of any passion whatsoever, the following are the earliest two letters that Susan and I wrote to each other; the first two of the 85 letters that Susan saved. Mine is postmarked July 12, 1957, from the Manhattan Hotel, where we first met. Hers is dated September 22, 1958. It is the innocence of these letters that makes them all the more precious.

Undoubtedly we were in contact between the dates of these letters. I returned to the Bronx after my summer job ended and we then communicated by phone and in person until I left for my freshman year at Boston University in September, 1958. Because it is the first letter I ever got from her, I cherish it, and in particular because it is signed "Love Susan." This was the first time that a girl used the word "love" to me. Up to this point I'd had other girlfriends: There was Arlene, Judy, Cassie, and Joan, plus there were Julie and Linda who I hung out with in the neighborhood. Only one of these earlier girlfriends struck a chord in me to want a deeper connection, which she did not want, and so we broke up. None of them ever used the word "love"; neither did I. When I wrote this first letter to Susan, I had just started my freshman year of college. I was 17, she was 15.

Dear Susan,

How are you? I'm pretty good (except that I miss the way you annoyed me—in a nicely annoying way). You don't have to worry about my being a good boy, I'm always a good boy (maybe that's the trouble). The weather has been fairly cool up here since you left; or maybe it was your sunny disposition that kept it pleasant while you were here. There isn't much more to tell right now except that I am hoping to see you in the very near future. (Don't forget to write)

Love,
Bob

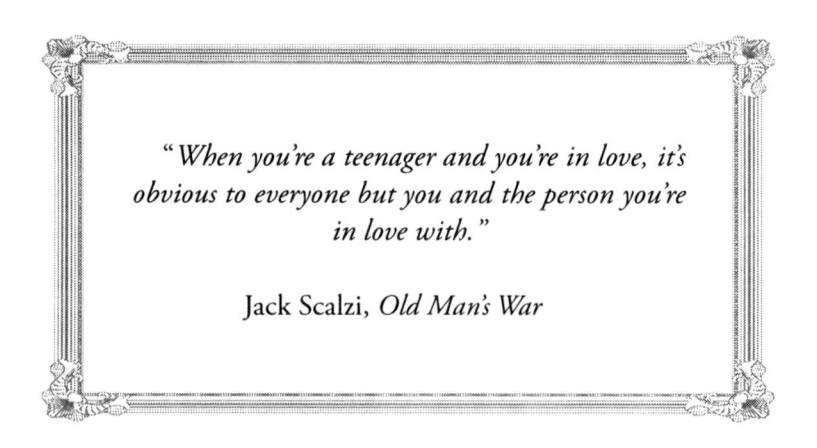

> "When you're a teenager and you're in love, it's obvious to everyone but you and the person you're in love with."
>
> Jack Scalzi, *Old Man's War*

And her first letter to me.

Dear Bob,

Everyone here is fine. What are you taking up in college? I haven't taken any pictures yet, so you'll have to be patient. Could you send me a picture of the boy I am writing to? Do you go to the movies often out there, because there aren't many good pictures here. Did you get a chance to meet girls? My girlfriend went up to the Manhattan Hotel and she said that they all expected you up there. You should know her, her name is Muriel. She was up there at the same time I was. She has black hair and a crooked nose. Did you ever hear from or speak to the boys that were in the band? I never saw any or spoke to any after that. Thank God. I guess that's all for now, because I'm fresh out of thoughts. Please write back soon.

Love,
Susan

It became a recurring theme in our exchange of letters for me to ask for a photo of her and for her to make excuses for not sending one.

My speculation as to the reason for this is that she did not consider herself to be pretty, which was strange to me because she was indeed a very pretty girl. This latter point of speculation intersects with another part of the story.

Chapter 31

Everyone Saw Her Angel Wings

I was looking through Susan's 1960 high school yearbook, her senior year. I don't know if kids still do this, but in those days, when a high school senior got his or her yearbook with all the photos of the graduates, they would go around asking friends to write something next to their photos in the yearbook.

Many people signed Susan's yearbook and it wasn't difficult to tell who was an acquaintance and who knew her better. Because it was an all girls high school there were many notes signed "love", not what you'd find in a typical note from adolescent boys, especially from one guy to another guy.

A strong thread in the comments written by people who knew her more than casually revealed that they all liked her a lot, had fun spending time with her, and considered her to be a "sweet" girl. Many wrote things like: "Stay as sweet as you are." I'd forgotten that I wrote something in her yearbook:

October 15, 1961
To My Dearest Susan,

Usually when someone signs a senior yearbook it is because you want a memento or a remembrance of a high school pal that you will probably lose contact with in the coming years. What I'm writing will be a memento also but one that we will share together.

If love could be measured in dollars and cents I'd be the richest man in the world. Here's wishing us the best of everything forever and ever. I love you very much.

Yours forever,
Bob

Chapter 32

A Dark Season

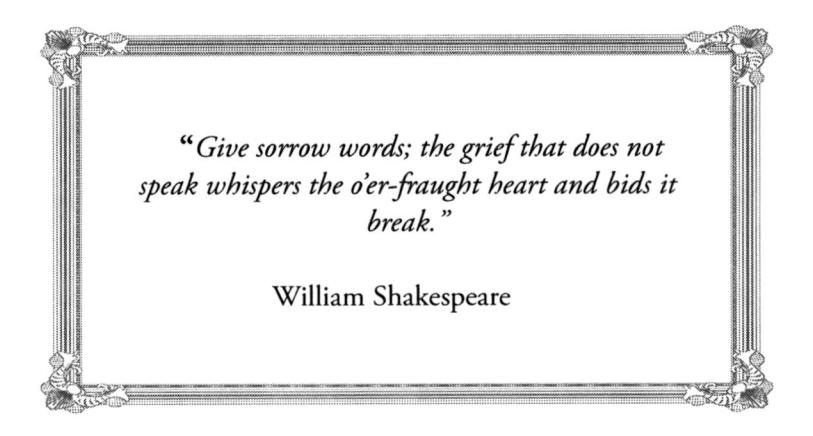

> *"Give sorrow words; the grief that does not speak whispers the o'er-fraught heart and bids it break."*
>
> William Shakespeare

I wrote the following letter to Susan in 1960, after she suddenly, and without any explanation, broke up with me on a phone call. We'd been dating for some time. I was stunned and shattered.

There has been no greater painful experience in my life, apart from her death. Yet it proved my love for her; at least it did for me. She celebrated her seventeenth birthday the month prior to the letter. So, this was about a year and a half after her first letter to me when I was at Boston University.

I would be 19 in a few months, living with my parents, commuting to New York University's Washington Square campus in lower Manhattan's Greenwich Village, in my sophomore year of college, having transferred there from Boston University. It wasn't long after this letter that I gained insight into the "why" that she never directly answered.

As I recently reread this letter for the first time in many years, I cried, just as I cried the first time that I read it. Obviously, Susan saved this letter, as well as all the letters we exchanged. I'm so glad that she saved these precious outpourings of our hearts.

March 23, 1960
Dear Susan,

You're probably very surprised to receive a letter from me, but I have a lot of things pent up inside me since—well—you know when. Please don't get the idea that I'm trying to haunt you by writing to you; I just feel that the best way to release my emotions under the circumstances is to write.

First of all, I still cannot figure out why you broke up with me so damn suddenly, and without any reason. (That's what you told me.) I know there are many boys that will go with a girl just to see how much they can get; as you probably know, I'm not like that. I really loved you Susan. I guess I always did—and I'm afraid I always will. When I told you how I felt, I meant it with all my heart. To me, you were everything. I lived for you. You were more important to me than anything in the world.

I knew you were a moody girl and I let you have your way. As far as I can recall, I never did anything to hurt you and I never lost my temper. I thought that if I was nice to you, you would change your ways a little and be more understanding toward me. But, I'm only human, and I was wrong.

I guess I had a feeling all along that you would get tired of me, but I disregarded it. I wanted you and I hoped that you wanted me. I needed you and I hoped that you needed me—I was wrong again. That night that I called you at your friend Susan's house is one conversation that I'll never forget. I can still remember your words exactly. I can truthfully say that I've never been hurt as much by anyone as I was by you that night.

Whether you realize it or not Susan, I have a hell of a lot of pride. There are very few people that I'd lower my pride for. You were on the top of the list. I begged you to reconsider that night. I never begged anyone for anything before in my life. You wouldn't even let me see you once more. And then to top it all off, you said I could have the ankle bracelet back. That was cruel, Susan. You could have kicked me in the teeth and it would have hurt less. And even then I didn't lose my temper. My love for you left no room for any other emotions.

I was all choked up and I said to myself—this isn't the same girl that I loved—how could she hurt me so deeply, and why couldn't she at least say it to my face? As soon as I hung up I went downstairs in a daze. I had a big lump in my throat, and I was fighting to hold back the tears that were swelling my eyes. And one big question kept popping up in my head—Why? Why? Why? I couldn't figure it out for my life. I went to bed early that night—still in a daze. I sat staring at the darkness in my room—still wondering why. Then I rolled over and—laugh if you want to—broke down crying.

I loved you so much and you didn't even give a damn whether I lived or died, is what I thought. This was too much for me to take. I couldn't control myself. That was only one of many nights I cried myself to sleep. There hasn't been a day or night since, that the thought of you and the good times we used to have, doesn't enter my mind—time after time after time, and always the same unanswered question—Why???

I sat down this morning and reread all of the letters you sent me when I was away at school last year. You used to write how much you missed me and how much you loved me and again I cried. All a bunch of lies, I said. She lied while I fell in love with her.

I've been wanting so much to call you since that day, but I couldn't take being hurt anymore. I used to drive by your house at night, hoping I might be satisfied by just catching a glimpse of you walking in the street. But that would only have made things worse. When you called about the party the other night I was overjoyed just to hear your voice again, as cold as it was. When you hung up it started all over again. The same lousy feeling came back even stronger now, and I knew then that I could never forget you.

I began to drink a lot the first few weeks after we broke up. That helped me to forget for a while, but it was only temporary peace. I would actually lie awake late at night and pray that you would come back to me, but that only made things worse. You broke my heart, Susan, but I still love you as much as I always did.

When I took Susan out Sunday, I knew that was you behind us in the hall. Susan didn't have to tell me, I sensed it, I really did. On the way home we spoke about you and me for quite a while. Please don't tell Susan (she's a very sweet girl) but, the real reason that I asked her out was to talk about you. I thought that talking about you with someone that knew you might help. Again, it helped for a while, but when I saw you that night, I knew that I still felt the same way. I wanted so much to talk to you, but I just froze for a second. Something inside me wouldn't let me say a word. I guess I didn't want to take a chance on being hurt anymore. I couldn't take it.

I didn't go straight home that night. I was very upset. I just rode around thinking about you. When I finally got home it was quite late and my mother was very worried and upset. My father was angry. He told me I couldn't use the car for a month. Ordinarily, this would have started a big argument, but I didn't even care. In fact I laughed. I sat and smoked a cigarette, and went to bed with the now familiar choked up feeling, and I cried.

I've done a lot of crying over you. The last time I really cried was when my grandmother died. I loved my grandmother very much. I should be studying for finals now but I can't concentrate. I'm a very confused boy. My picture of the world went out of focus and hasn't come back yet. I don't care about anything anymore. I just exist.

I guess it isn't all on the inside anymore either. When you called about Susan's party last week, my mother answered the phone. When I hung up, I went into my room and just stared out the window. My mother walked into the room and just stood there looking at me. Then she said—"You still like her, don't you?" I just stared at her. What could I say?

I suppose I've done quite a bit of writing. Call me a fool, call me stupid, call me anything you want. You can laugh at this letter, you can show it to anyone you want, I don't care. Every single word that I've written is what I truly feel. I meant every word of it, and

I'm not ashamed to admit it. Losing you hurt me more than you'll ever know. That's all that matters to me. I know it means nothing to you.

Just remember what I said to you that night over the phone—You'll never find anyone that loves you as much as I do. You'll always be the girl as far as I'm concerned. I have to live with the terrible hurt—you don't. But somehow I feel that I'm the lucky one and you aren't.

My heart is yours forever, but my love for you will have to remain in my dreams. I hope that you are happy. I want you to be happy. Think of me once in a while—I think of you constantly.

Bob

> "You will never know true happiness until you have truly loved, and you will never understand what pain really is until you have lost it."
>
> Anonymous

Chapter 33

Love Reborn

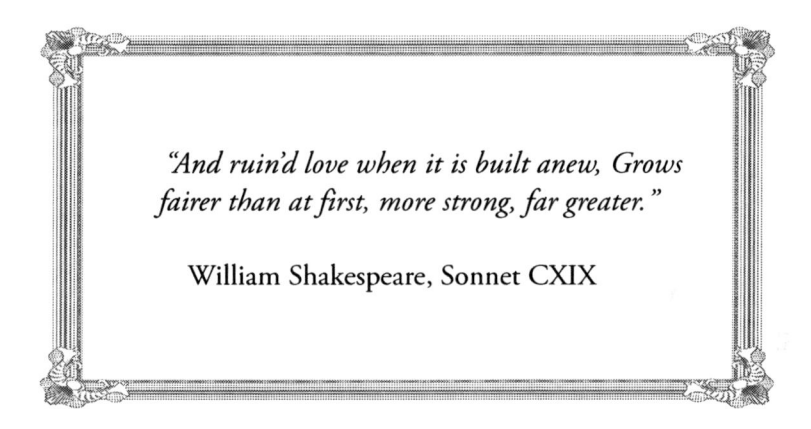

> *"And ruin'd love when it is built anew, Grows fairer than at first, more strong, far greater."*
>
> William Shakespeare, Sonnet CXIX

I did not recognize it then, but after Susan ended our relationship, I was experiencing gut-wrenching grief for a great loss in my life. It was as though Susan died to me for the first time in 1960.

Then, by the grace of God, things changed. The following may be the most precious letter that I've ever received. I've never shared it with anyone. Now, it's a banner of love-restored that I'd like to fly from the housetops. It was from Susan, dated February 9, 1961. She would celebrate her eighteenth birthday in a couple of weeks. I was going to be 20 in July. She wrote this letter on 3-hole, lined school notebook paper, one sheet, both sides. I cried reading this letter, even after so many years. I loved her so deeply.

Hi Lover,

Just thought I'd drop a line to tell you that I love you very much. Please forgive the paper, but I'm in school and that's all I have.

Bob, you can't realize how happy I've been these past months since we've been seeing each other again. When we first broke up, I really didn't think about you that much. After the summer I started longing for you again. I don't know why, but maybe you could say I've been used to seeing you during the winter months. I went out quite a bit after we broke up.

I've already told you about a boy named Steven. I really thought that I was in love with him. We were seeing each other for about four months. During that time I used to think about you often, and all the fun we used to have together. Do you know something, I didn't give him a reason either. He used to call me and ask me why; but I've never, even to this day, told him. I went out with a lot of other boys after that. I thought I liked them, but I really went out with them to forget about you. I was just trying to do the impossible. I knew then, that I really love you, and I finally called you.

Do you know that when we went out that Saturday after I first called you, I was crying. I was crying in the car going to Connecticut, crying in the movie theater, and crying going home. You probably couldn't tell, because I was crying inside. The kind of crying I did every night for you. I used to try to kill myself in my sleep. I'd think of ways to kill myself. I'd try to hold my breath until I'd die, but, I don't know why, I just couldn't. Maybe it was because I'd pray that there was still some hope for us, and that kept me alive.

Well, I'm very glad I had that little spark of hope, because my prayers were answered.

I can't recall her ever referring to me as "Lover" either before or after this letter, or at any time during our marriage. I loved it!

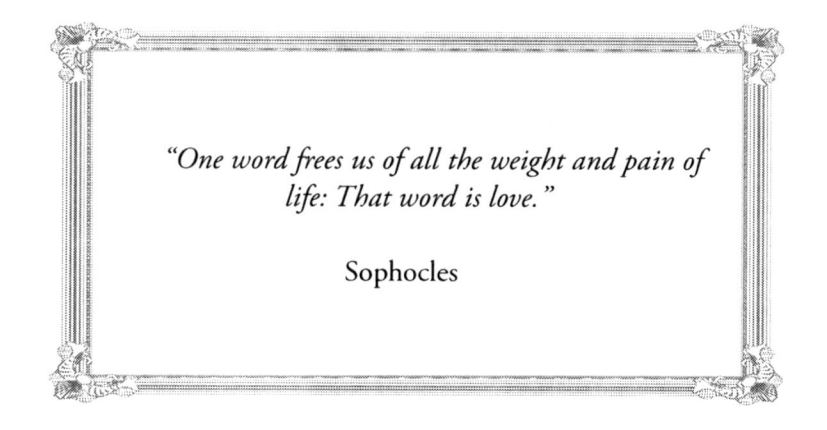

> *"One word frees us of all the weight and pain of life: That word is love."*
>
> Sophocles

This expression of love and happiness about which Susan wrote to me illustrates and emphasizes simple, yet precious words after our relationship had deepened and matured. Many of the earliest letters would probably be very boring reading for folks other than Susan and me. Sixteen year old boys, and fourteen year old girls in the 1950s were a lot more innocent and naive than today's generation of teens. A sad reality.

Think about it. We were actually writing to each other, using pen and paper, and then walking to a mail box and mailing the letters through the United Stated Postal Service, using four cent postage stamps that were not peel-offs . . . you had to lick the nasty dried glue on the back. These desperately awaited communications took days to arrive. There was no other way to communicate for our generation other than on the telephone, or face-to-face, which was cost-prohibitive while I was attending Boston University and she was at home in New York City.

No personal computers even existed yet, nor pocket electronic devices of any kind, and no cell phones. No texting. No Facebook or any such social networking. No blogs. What kind of horrible world did I grow up in?

Trust me: It wasn't bad at all. In fact, it was very good. When it's all you know, it's all you know. Get it? It simply meant that communications were likely to be more thoughtful because it takes more time to hand-write a letter, and, you can't hit "Send" before it's more polished by rereading it a few times to change things that need changing, or you just pitch it and start over on a clean sheet of paper. We learned to be patient. We learned to look into each other's faces and talk with one another close up, not hide behind the barriers of clever electronics. We learned to listen. We learned to speak real, complete words and sentences to each other, rather than typed abbreviations and codes. (Go ahead, LOL.)

There were no instant photos or movies readily taken with slick pocket devices, shared with half the people in the universe at the press of a button. How often today do we hear horror stories about foolish teens who sent compromising photos of themselves 'privately' to so-called friends, after which, perhaps in just moments, the pictures go viral on the internet? Today, a teen's future life trajectory can be negatively altered in the blink of an eye depending on who may see revealing pictures of drunk teen girls, and equally crude and thoughtless postings by boys. For those foolish enough to keep such 'mementos' on their social networking sites, beware the savvy job recruiters who now regularly explore the social networking sites of job applicants.

When Susan and I got together with friends, we actually got together . . . a group of real live people in the same room at the same time, looking at each other, talking to one another, playing cards or board games, listening to music without individual headsets, connecting on a personal, three-dimensional, real-time, flesh and blood level. Today it is not uncommon to see young people texting back and forth while in the same room with each other, and children fussing with their handhelds while at a restaurant table with their families, oblivious to the people around them. Is this progress for humanity? Draw your own conclusions.

Chapter 34

All My Love All My Love

The following letter from Susan is dated November 30, 1961, while we were courting . . . now there's an ancient word for you: "courting"! Do you suppose that young people today have any clue as to what "courtship" means? I have my doubts. So, just in case some youngster is reading this (probably as a parental punishment), I'll save him or her a Google or whatever the most current search-in-a-microsecond mechanism is: Courtship means: "to seek another's love", according to my hard cover, three pound dictionary. At the time she wrote this letter Susan was approaching 19 years old. I was 20. We were now adults. Being playful, she addressed it to:

Mr. Robert S. Duchin

I love you very much. I know that you love me too. I've just finished reading all the letters you've ever written to me, . . . they were beautiful. I'm saving every one of them to read to our children. We should get together one of these days and read them back and forth. It should be fun.

While you were away at Boston, you'd always request a picture of me in practically every single letter you wrote. Well, being that I never sent any to you then, I'm enclosing some now (only 15). Practically every picture I have of myself. All for you because I love you so much and also because I was very selfish to you.

I think that I've just begun to realize how rotten I used to treat you. I know I've said it before, but I'll say it again, I'm really truly and deeply sorry for all the hurt I've ever caused you.

I'll never stop saying I love you, so don't try to tame me down. (Taming of the Shrew?)

All My Love All My Love
Susan

Almost exactly two years later we were married, and left our respective parents' homes for the first time in our lives, to begin our own lives together.

It was also an intervention and a rescue that I could barely wait to activate. The love of my life was deeply injured. I'd learned the extent of it before we were married. I hoped that my love and our marriage could help to bring healing.

Chapter 35

Married At Last

After a large, formal, catered wedding, with serving tables overflowing with hors d'oeuvres, a live orchestra, full dinner, the whole deal, we were off to our honeymoon on the beautiful island of Bermuda. Neither of us had ever been outside the U.S., and Susan had never flown on an airplane until our honeymoon flight! By the way, there were no jet passenger planes yet. Our flight was on a four engine propeller driven plane, nice for its day, but you could hear it coming 100 miles away and the cabin vibration could dislocate your joints.

Fortunately, Bermuda is not that far from New York City, just a few hundred miles off the coast of North Carolina. Our long-awaited wedding night was anticlimactic, no pun intended . . . Susan had what she called her monthly "visitor". Nature sometimes has a quirky and untimely sense of humor.

Nonetheless, we had a fantastic and memorable time, riding motor bikes all over the island, eating in English pubs, exploring the stunning pink sand beaches, swimming in the pristine, blue-green ocean waters, enjoying the commonly occurring tropical showers that blew in and out in just a few minutes, and buying some lovely mementos for our new home.

Susan had a little trouble getting the hang of navigating turns on the motor bike, so we found a school with a circular driveway where she practiced turning for a while until she was confident enough to take to the roads. The children were in class while we used their driveway, and they hung out the windows waving to us. At one end of the island Susan was concentrating so intently on keeping on the correct side of the road—the left side (Bermuda was a British island)—that she rode right past a sign indicating to stay out because it was the entrance to a prison. This really shook her up and it really cracked me up.

We returned to New York City excited to occupy our first apartment as a married couple, in Queens County. (New York City's five boroughs are each a separate county.) Our apartment in Queens was located less than a half hour drive from our former homes in the Bronx, across the graceful Whitestone Bridge. We didn't own a car until we'd been married for almost three years, so our parents and friends would come to visit us. You just didn't need a car in New York City unless it was necessary for your job, because the public transportation was so accessible and inexpensive. Susan and I were both working, and we commuted by bus and subway from our new home to our jobs in Manhattan, about an hour commute each way. No big deal . . . we were two of hundreds of thousands of folks who did the same thing Monday through Friday every work week.

The subways were wretchedly stifling during the summer months. No air-conditioned subway cars existed until the World's Fair was to be located in New York. Then, magically, the old subway cars that would transport visitors to the World's Fair site were replaced with shiny new air-conditioned cars. We were fortunate enough to get the benefit of this because of where we lived.

We used cash wedding gifts to furnish our small apartment. It was plenty big enough for the two of us and we loved being on our own, together. All our furniture was bought at wholesale prices because everyone in New York City knows somebody, who knows somebody, who sells this or that wholesale. Our parents were no exception to the rule and so we applied my mother's wisdom: "Buy the best that you can afford." I remember the salesman who waited on us in the furniture showroom when we were looking at a pricey sofa, at least it was pricey for us. He convinced us of how strongly it was built by removing the seat cushions and then getting on it and jumping up and down. We were impressed! We bought it.

Wedding Profile

Wedding Dance

Chapter 36

Dreaded Reality: 100 Days

A letter I wrote to friends and relatives 100 days after Susan died.

~ ~ ~ ~ ~ ~ ~ ~ ~ ~ ~

It is hard to believe that it's been 100 days since my sweet Susan took her last breath in front of my horrified eyes in her quiet hospital room. I feel that I want to commemorate this in some small way by sharing a synopsis of the journey thus far.

This is partly selfish of me because "talking" about Susan keeps her memory more alive to me. Yet I also hope that as long as you are willing to make the sacrifice necessary to share my grief with me at some level, you might internalize the wisdom contained in the Biblical proverb that fundamentally states: That it is better to visit a house of mourning than a house of feasting, for death comes to all of us, therefore consider the things most important in life.

Now that I have a broader perspective after 100 days, where am I now, emotionally, spiritually, and physically?

Some ask me: Are you doing any better? I appreciate people's concern for me but I don't know how to answer this question because there's no baseline of comparison except what my life was like before Susan died. Everyone's journey of grieving the loss of a loved one is unique, so the experts say. After this first 100 days I have come to believe this to be true.

Compared to before Susan died, then, am I doing better?

How could I be doing better than when the love of my life for 54 years is no longer my constant companion as a devoted wife for 47 of those 54 years, forgiver of all my insensitivities and dumb mistakes, mother of my children, grandmother to five little ones who probably will not remember her, or the bottomless maternal love that she gave so freely, my confidante, my lover, my sounding board, my conscience, my household and financial manager, a cook extraordinaire . . .

I'm not doing 'better', I'm doing 'differently'.

Life doesn't take a time-out because my world happened to be turned upside down and inside out . . . I have to do things differently or suffer the consequences of neglected health and day-to-day responsibilities. Have I gotten a handle on managing my household? Much to my relief I have, for the most part. There are still glitches that are occurring such as an overlooked property tax payment a few months ago. The invoice was in with our income tax papers and it got lost in the shuffle; and a missed mortgage payment too. I've been able to bring things current but not without having to dig a hole in my retirement savings. Yet I am blessed that even though these financial surprises deplete my retirement fund at a more rapid rate, at least I still have the resources to cover such occurrences.

Emotionally?

I was concerned that I would not be able to cry after Susan died. After the first 100 days there may be only one day, though my memory is fuzzy, during which tears did not come. The tear-triggers are still devastatingly hidden, tripped with little if any warning most times. The instances of uncontrollable sobbing have diminished and so I wonder if I'm grieving poorly because the terrible peaks of grief have subsided somewhat. I know that this is irrational thinking but I'm not in a fully rational state these days. This is not a game and I shouldn't be a scorekeeper, and yet I feel as though I should be crying every day. Sometimes I can bring myself to tears very easily by choosing what I want to picture in my mind, especially Susan's appearance in her last hours. Crazy, isn't it?

Sometimes it's just tearful moments off and on throughout the day. Sometimes I just find myself quietly moaning with no tears but with just as much pain in my heart. I don't know if the pain is diminishing or if I'm just getting more accustomed to it. I pray that it's the former not the latter.

I often wake in the morning thinking that I hear Susan puttering in the kitchen. One time I realized that some branches touching the rain gutters were making a rustling sound when blown by the wind and the sound was being echoed through the inside of the house, reinforcing my belief that someone was moving about here or there. Not being fully awake, it scared me, sensing that Susan was still with me, and then the shock and the disappointment, after becoming more fully awake, that it was only an imagined desire. On such days I arise from bed already let down as the long day begins.

I've done some redecorating primarily in our bedroom. Curtains on the windows where there were only shutters; new bedding. Shifting some wall hangings and lamps from one room or wall to another. It's surprising to me how much you can change a look without spending much money. This refreshing of our bedroom has also helped me to sort of put a new stamp on what was our space, and now must be accepted as my space.

I still wear my wedding ring with a cross, on a chain around my neck, and this continues to feel ok to me.

For a while I slept on Susan's side of the bed because it was too painful for me to wake up every day, or in the middle of the night, and see and feel the emptiness in the space that she occupied for so long. Surprisingly, this shift helped, so I continued to do this until I felt it no longer plugged the hole that I was trying to fill. I'm now back on my side of the bed.

I've spent a lot of time sorting through old photos . . . three cartons full. This was bittersweet, as you might imagine. I've sorted the photos and intend to pass the pictures on to each of my children, plus some for Susan's brother, my brother, and some other folks who I know will value them.

There were some photos of Susan that I remembered vividly and that I especially treasured. I was worried that they might have been lost. Well, thank God! Not only did I find the photos, but for several of my most favorite ones, I also found the negatives! I've had these photos cleaned up by a photo studio and have not yet decided how to display some of them.

Some of these pictures of Susan I scanned into my computer for safekeeping, and I've got them on my desktop so that every time I open my computer, the pictures are the first thing I see. They never fail to cheer me and so this is good medicine for my heart and soul.

I gave up Susan's Disabled Person license plates replacing them with personalized plates. This was another event which triggered deeper sadness because it is just one of many events that punctuate the fact that she's gone and things must change.

Spiritually?

This is what I believe: God is still God, the same yesterday, today and forever. He is sovereign over all people and things no matter how incomprehensible our life events may appear to us. You don't have to agree with this. I'm just telling you where I'm coming from.

Susan's last words to me were: "I did this to myself." Whether she meant it to help me or not I'll never know, but it may have contributed to my not—at least to this moment—blaming God for her suffering and death. I've been drawn closer to God as my harshly shaken life changed so quickly and so radically. Where else does one who professes

Jesus Christ as Lord and Savior turn when unthinkable events suddenly occur? I suppose some may turn away from God at such times, and this, in my opinion, is tragedy on top of tragedy.

This has been far and away the greatest test of my faith in my life and I hope and pray that similar things will not happen to me again in my lifetime, though one cannot have any such assurance. As unbearable as things have been, God is my firm anchor. I thank Him for being both the Almighty God and the All-Merciful God, and though His ways are too high for me to fully understand, I do understand and thank Him for this: Susan and I had 47 wonderful years together, she did not suffer long, and I believe that she is now in God's Heaven, with no more pain or fear, rejoicing constantly in His very presence. This wonderful picture often carries me over some nasty crevices in my daily landscape. And, if that were not good enough reason for seeing some joy amidst my ordeal, I also know that I will someday see my sweet Susan again when we reunite in Heaven.

Physically?

The full load of all the household responsibilities takes its toll on my arthritic condition, which flares more often but, thank God, has not been severe except on a few occasions. I take more meds when it's acute, and physical therapy off and on, which helps too. I've been trying to get back into my exercise routine. This has been difficult after a break of four months but I'm working on it and trying to not overdo it so that I can avoid physical inflammations and injuries.

Surprisingly to me, my appetite is good and thanks to sweet Susan's shopaholic addiction, I'm still chipping away at food she stored in our freezers. I've even ventured to try cooking a couple of our favorite recipes—actually the recipes are my mother's: meat loaf and cod fish cakes. I was pleased with the results and I'm sure that Susan would be proud of me and had a big smile on her face while I was messing around in the kitchen, reading her faded, handwritten, food-stained recipe cards over and over again to be sure I wasn't screwing things up.

Little things trigger explosive anger at times, like when I break a glass or a dish, or accidentally drop and spill something. I'm learning to be more patient with life and now, when things like this occur, instead of cussing about it, I've begun to say out loud: "But, I can do it." Meaning, that thanks to God, I still have the physical ability to get out of bed and perform most daily tasks without any assistance, including otherwise insignificant things like sweeping up broken glass and wiping up spilled liquids.

I'm not getting much sleep and my doctor is concerned that I'm going to crash. I'm taking meds for anxiety and depression, adding a little extra at bedtime, and I also added Melatonin a couple of weeks ago. So far, not much change. Surprisingly I usually awake not feeling too tired even when I get only four hours sleep, which is typical.

Another thing the experts state, and which I believe, is that there is no such thing as 'recovery' from terrible losses like the death of a spouse. One author says that it is more like an amputation than any other medical analogy. A part of me is cut off and gone permanently. Life suddenly changed for me and will never be the same again. I need to surrender to the reality and the magnitude of the loss and choose how to cope with it.

Susan's memory will always prompt both sadness and joy. As time moves on I hope that the joyful memories will weigh more heavily on the balance scales than they do right now.

This tragic loss will forever change the way I relate to my God, my children, my grandchildren, my friends, and in fact everyone with whom I come into contact. Hopefully some greater good will come out of the legacy of my life with Susan.

Chapter 37

More Love Letters

As I've been considering what to write about our lives together, I began mulling over the idea of writing a goodbye letter to Susan because we did not have a chance to have a goodbye conversation; she became comatose so quickly. This sad fact caused a deeper crack in my broken heart at the time and still dredges up considerable sadness.

Then I remembered that besides the love letters of our teen years that Susan saved, bless her dear heart, there were letters that I wrote to her on special occasions when we were well into our married lives. In rereading these letters that I saved, I found in them the very expression of many of the things I would have wanted to tell her again if we'd had the chance to talk with each other one last time before she passed away from my reality. I hope that somehow these words were in her mind as she lay unconscious before me.

I am so sorry that I did not get one final opportunity to look into her beautiful blue eyes and remind her that all the words and sentiments I wrote to her in these letters were, and still are, the deepest truths of my heart. I'm sharing them now without a single change in any of the content of these love letters. Not because I feel that they have great literary merit. Because I want you to know her as the exceptional woman that she was, and how I wanted to then, and still do now, honor her life's great accomplishments in the things that really matter. The things that she intuitively knew were of the greatest importance, long before I arrived at that place in my own heart. I had a college degree. Susan was my professor of real life.

Mother's Day, Sunday, May 12th, 2002

To My Dear Wife,

You have been through tribulation in your life that might have resulted in your being a poor mother or perhaps even not being desirous of having children of your own. Yet somehow you not only wanted to have your own children, but you also became the most wonderful mom to all three of our beautiful offspring.

Often, in the early years, without the kind of support from me that you should have had, you somehow managed to fill the gap and provide extraordinary love and devotion to our children. I've wondered how or from whom you learned how to do things so right, and I'm at a loss to explain it in human terms.

Perhaps God, even before you knew Him, determined to put within you a heart of unfailing love and devotion for your children, and for your husband. Whatever the reason, the result was and continues to be something that I am so grateful for: Children who have always and who continue to know the unconditional and bottomless well of healthy love of their unique and dear mother.

So, you deserve to be recognized, applauded, and deeply loved for accomplishing something truly great and rare in our family: Three wonderful children who always knew and still do that they were protected, comforted and loved, loved, loved by their special mom.

And I love you ever more deeply for this part of who you are.

Happy Mother's Day
Bob

Our 40th Wedding Anniversary 2003

Dearest Susan,

Looking through your high school yearbook with you simply confirmed things about you that are so true. People long forgotten by you, who at a point in your young life, when you thought not much of yourself, recognized your specialness. Your sweet spirit was something that evidently shone through in spite of what may have been happening in your own mind and in your life.

My own words written in your yearbook then could be my very words today, more than 40 years later. You have managed to overcome great adversity in your life without permitting your experiences to embitter you. You determined to be as good a wife and mother as you possibly could be in spite of the lack of encouragement and modeling in your early years. Somehow you taught yourself how to do it, and do it well you did…and you still do.

You are a joy. My love and appreciation for you grows daily even after all these years—and maybe even more so after all these years. Why? Because you have been a triumphant example of sacrificial love—towards an undeserving and unappreciative me, and to our wonderful three children … and you continue to be, day-in and day-out. Nothing seems to overshadow your ability to love!

My stubbornness and my hardness of heart can only melt before your tenderness. How truly blessed I am that you are my wife…my mate…my comfort…my dear love.

I can only attempt to express how much I love, need and admire you, in these inadequate few words. I will try to become more worthy of your love, although I will probably fail, and yet I know that you will probably love me no less for my failure. How I wish I could be more like you. Our blessed God most certainly gave me the most special person when He gave me you as my wife. I am so happy to be celebrating our 40th Wedding Anniversary together. I love you sweet Susan!

Bob

On Her Birthday, February 25th, 2006

Dearest Susan,

Your friends at work are so right to celebrate the day you were born. So do I! Because, the day you were born, God promised you to me to be my wife, and His blessing in doing so is immeasurable.

I love you more than I can put into words. You are so lovable! Your spirit of kindness, forgiveness, hospitality and genuine heartfelt, God-led care for others sets you apart, as others clearly recognize. Yours are special gifts from God, and those around you, especially me, are so deeply blessed to be recipients of your presence and the way you so unselfishly give of yourself. So, I too celebrate the birth of my precious wife, a gift to me every day of the year! I will do my best to make this day a happy day for you, it is the least I can do in exchange for the comfort and joy I find in your presence.

With deep love and respect for who you are,
Bob

Our 45th Wedding Anniversary 2008

Dear Susan,

Every day in so many small ways you reflect the love you so freely give to me. Your warm smile, asking how well I slept the night before, cooking the things I like, allowing me to choose what we watch on TV, going with me to do things you may not be too excited about, reading articles I push your way, buying things at the food markets that I like, wanting my kisses and hugs. And there are big ways too. Like the way you love and still care for our children. Your way of loving is still remarkable to me. I wish I could be as good at it as you are. So in my small ways I want to emphasize how much I love you, and how glad I am that we've been together in love for all these 45 years. I hope and pray there are many more years to come.

With much love and admiration for you, a truly special child of God.

Love today and always,
Bob

Four short months before she died

Happy 47th Anniversary to My Beloved Wife
2010

Dearest Susan,

More and more each day I grow to realize and value the precious fact that you are the most important person in my life. Not just because I've come to need you, though I surely do need you, but more because of your spirit that is as sweet and pure as any spirit I've ever been touched by. Your spirit is like no elixir imaginable.

I'm not suggesting that you are without imperfection, for who is? Yet, all in all, when the balance scale is brought out, your tenderness, patience, warmth, desire to serve others with joy, and your seemingly unlimited forgiving heart, are but a few of the wonderfully special and high characteristics that far outweigh any imperfections. This is what makes you the person I deeply love, and I yearn to love you more like you love me.

So you are a model for the most important characteristics that I believe set certain marriages apart from others and therefore make them last. I aspire to be more like the standard you set. Though I may never attain it, I thank God every day for you and pray that I might someday be as good at loving you as you are at loving me.

Thank you for accepting me, for being unwavering in your mercy toward me, and for being my most wonderful wife for 47 years.

With much love and admiration,
Bob

Chapter 38

Unexpected Intersection

I'm not finished with grieving, not by a long shot, even now ten months since my sweet Susan suddenly died.

I'm the kind of person who is wired to need and dig for answers. I've learned a lot about grief so far and knowing more has been helpful for me. Here's some of what I've learned, and that I accept as truth.

In order for grief to end, or at least for it to become an irregularly reoccurring, non-dominating part of life following the devastating loss of a loved one, it must be permitted to run its course. I suppose that it's much like a severe wound that causes great pain and suffering for a time, must be treated intentionally and carefully to prevent complications, will never completely heal, yet at some point slowly diminishes to an occasional flareup causing manageable shorter bursts of distress.

I witnessed the result of untreated grief-avoidance many years ago, though at the time I had no conscious idea what was really going on. In retrospect it was a sad and terrible life experience. Not just for the grief-stricken persons, but also for those in their inner circle, especially immediate family members, and most especially young children who have no grasp whatsoever of what has happened and how it will affect their future lives.

The impacts of grief are circumscribed as relatively smaller or bigger scars on our lives based largely on how we choose and seek equipping to cope with it. We can either face it head-on until the worst of it has passed by, or we can try to outrun it in futility. This might be like someone in the eye of a tornado, terrified, yet with a false sense of safety because of the unnatural calm. Oh, if only this calm will last forever! But in every direction he looks, the turbulent storm surrounds and whirls around him, and the eye of temporary safety is steadily moving away from him while the turbulent edge of the storm draws closer and closer.

Then, the only choices are to either voluntarily enter the reality of the situation by seeking shelter to diminish risk, or waiting for it to sweep over you, or worse, to sweep you up and away with its raw power, and the distinct possibility of severe injury or death.

Trying to get on with life can feel like an insurmountable task when a person is already substantially diminished emotionally, spiritually, and physically, due to shock, anguish, anger, and fear. It is a dreaded and indeed dreadful part of life that most of us will be faced with at least once in our time on Earth. As if once is not more than enough!

I've come to a conscious awareness recently that the death of my beloved, sweet wife, Susan, is not the first time I've encountered and been irreparably impacted by grief for a loved one. The road has been a long one for me, and so I recently arrived at this place I call an intersection of griefs. I would not and did not consciously set out to find this intersection, but I am not in control of much (if anything at all) that life presents to me. The only control I have is: How will I respond?

Chapter 39

My First Grief

In July 1941 identical twin boys, Michael Howard, and me, Robert Stephen, were unexpectedly born to Fay and Richard "Dick" Duchin. By unexpectedly, I mean that a single child was expected by the doctor until the actual delivery. Amazing, huh!

In those days there were no regularly administered ultrasounds to track the micro-development of unborn children; there were no special diets and super prenatal vitamins for pregnant women; there weren't dozens of do's and don'ts, as is typical today. The mystery and amazement of conception and pregnancy was wonderful and exciting in a much more natural way. And most children were actually born normal and healthy!

Robert ("Bobby"), and Michael, were born 14 minutes apart, Michael being the older of the twins, each weighing in at a whopping four-something pounds. Tiny but totally healthy.

Bobby (left) and Michael Duchin

158 | *R.S. Duchin*

Twins July 1944

    To say that Fay and Dick Duchin were surprised and unprepared for twins would be a gross understatement. They were barely prepared for one child—their first—let alone two at the same time. They took it in stride though, perhaps in large part because Fay's mother, Sarah, Sarah's sister Rosie, who never married, and Fay's younger of her two sisters, Elaine, all lived together just two blocks away. They became a significant part of the help needed to care for these twin babies. This was the natural way that families functioned at the time: families lived in close proximity and were tightly interwoven in one another's lives.

Caring for babies in the 1940s was considerably more time consuming and labor intensive than it is today. There were no disposable diapers . . . cotton cloth diapers were used and secured with large, sharp, steel safety pins to hold them in place, and then the dirty diapers were accumulated in a hamper for a diaper cleaning service to take them away and bring a clean batch. There was no premixed, ready-to-go sterile formula to feed to infants. Formula was prepared from scratch and the glass bottles and rubber nipples had to be sterilized at home in boiling water as often as necessary.

Count the number of typical infant feedings every day, multiply by two, and you'll have the picture of a nearly constant sterilizer bubbling away on the small kitchen gas stovetop, during the middle of the hot, humid, New York City summer, in a one bedroom apartment, with no air conditioning, and a mother in constant motion.

Dick Duchin worked as a medical supplies salesman and was typically out of the house in the morning by 7:00 am, and home each day by 3:00 or 4:00 pm to do his paperwork. Dinner was served every night at 6:00 pm sharp. Dick ate by the clock: ask him if he was hungry and the first thing he'd do is look at his watch. I often do this today and it drives me nuts . . . and makes me smile.

The Duchins lived in a one bedroom, one bath apartment in a Bronx, New York, rent-controlled, six story, solid brick apartment building that was typical in New York City at that time; still is! The building had around 75 apartments. The entry lobby was columned, the marble floor richly colored in brown and black geometric patterns, the stairways and hallways on every floor were fully ceramic-tiled, the steps had solid white marble treads, and the apartments had solid plaster walls, solid wood parquet flooring, and patterned black and white, ceramic mini-tiled floors in the bathrooms. These structures were built with great care, and built to last, inside and out.

The Duchin's apartment windows on the second floor of the building faced the side alley from the single kitchen window, with an eye-level view of other apartment windows facing theirs, 15 feet away across the narrow alley. The building's back alleyway was the landscape view from the bedroom and living room windows. The back alley paralleled the long, black-tarred, flat rooftop of the single-story commercial establishments that lined the next street to the west, which fronted the subway tracks that were elevated in this part of the city. Trains were frequently traveling to points south and north within the city. Their sound was impossible to ignore for a stranger or the occasional visitor but became virtually unheard by the building occupants. It's amazing how the brain adapts and can shut out unpleasant things, real or imagined.

At some point the twins were given the bedroom, and Fay and Dick slept on a sofa bed in the living room, which they did for about five or six years until they were fortunate enough to get to the top of the waiting list for a two bedroom, one bath apartment in the same building. The new fifth floor apartment's bedroom windows faced the front of the building, directly across the street from Public School #105, the neighborhood public elementary school that still operates today. This new apartment was a big step up for the family, no pun intended.

Fay was a wonderful, natural, utterly dedicated mother. Her mother, Sarah, was likewise a warm and delightful woman, and younger sister Elaine, a teenager at this time, was wired the same way. Family was paramount to these women, including Fay's other, older sister, Gussie, who lived not as close by, but not too far away.

Fay was a wise and intelligent woman who, although she had no formal education beyond high school, was well-informed and articulate, had an intuitive and clear perception of the world around her, read people quickly and accurately, loved to dress well and look well put together—as much as she could while caring for twin infants 24/7—and loved social interactions with friends. She was a friend for life to those with whom she connected, and could be a formidable foe to those whom she mistrusted.

Dick had one sibling, his younger sister Sylvia, who also lived in the Bronx but not close by. Dick's father, Abraham Duchin, was a kindly, gentle, warmhearted man who worked his entire life as a tailor. He always dressed nattily and the Duchins never had to pay a penny for clothing alterations until grandpa Aby died in his 80s.

Dick was gregarious but not inclined to intimacy and only had one reasonably close friend, Sam Grosky, who lived with his family only a block away. Unfortunately, Sammy died in his 50s, while Dick lived in relatively good health until 93.

Dick loved to clown around with people, especially teasing, and seemed to always gravitate toward children when adult friends and their families got together. He was simply uncomfortable acting as an adult in an adult world. He was not so much a dreamer; he was an avoider.

Dick was well educated, having attended The Cooper Union, in New York City, graduating with certification in architecture. Though he never worked professionally as an architect, his natural drawing skill was a valuable asset designing custom medical equipment for business clients.

In contrast, Fay was a realist and a confronter. Not a confronter in a negative context. She simply faced problems and issues head-on to get them resolved. She was naturally inquisitive, well-spoken, and enjoyed keeping active physically even well into her late senior years. She performed in amateur theatrical shows. She loved to dance. She loved to swim. She loved to cook and oh my, could she cook! She knitted and crocheted masterfully. When she spoke on the phone with her sisters, which was often, the conversations could last seemingly forever. I often wondered what folks who spoke with each other and saw each other so often could find to talk about that could possibly last more than a couple of minutes . . . a guy thing, right?

Dick was not a confronter and not a realist. He had a tight and narrow view of his world. His job was to work each day to provide for his family. Period. He had no significant hobbies or recreational interests except for his and Fay's frequent socializing with friends, all of whom lived within walking distance, and who most of the time would get together in each others' apartments to play poker and shmooze. These were strictly working middle-class families who lived within their means, and whose lives were routine, but not boring. Just about all moms during this era were stay-at-home moms. Although Fay worked before she was married, she did not have a paying job again until all her children were out of the house and well established in their own lives. Then she took a part-time job in a neighborhood drugstore just to have something to do and to interact with people.

The neighborhood that the Duchins lived in, "Pelham Parkway," was one of the finest in New York City for middle-class families. The apartment buildings in this area were erected in the 1930s, and so, when Dick and Fay moved there it was a brand new neighborhood in a part of New York City that 25 years earlier had still been very rural. It was about a 30 minute subway ride (for 15 cents!) to midtown Manhattan, a five minute walk to Bronx Park—an enormous, beautiful, free playground for these fortunate city kids, and a 20 minute walk to the Bronx Zoo and the New York Botanical Gardens. It was a great place to live and to raise a family. As it turned out, and I don't really know the reason, from the 1940s through the 1970s, the neighborhood called "Pelham Parkway" was probably 90% or more Jewish.

Anything that neighborhood folks needed was available within a three or four block walking radius: groceries, live poultry and live fish in the markets, Jewish delicatessens, Chinese, Greek, and Italian restaurants, clothing and furniture stores, banks, movie theaters, synagogues . . . you name it, you could walk to it. A car was a luxury and was not needed unless a person required one for their job, as Dick Duchin did. The public transportation in New York City was so good and so inexpensive that you could get to just about anywhere in the city for 15 cents and in an hour or less.

I remember taking the subway with friends to travel from Pelham Parkway in the Bronx, to Coney Island in Brooklyn, to spend the day on the boardwalk and beach, and to enjoy the amusement park rides, including at the time, three roller coasters. This trip across New York City, including passage under the East River from Manhattan to Brooklyn, took almost two hours each way, and with free transfers to various subway trains, cost 15 cents each way.

Life was good for the Pelham Parkway Duchins. Until 1945. The twins, Bobby and Michael, were then three years old.

Michael became lethargic and sickly. After a number of medical consults Michael was diagnosed with leukemia. No treatment was prescribed. Presumably there was no available treatment at the time. The doctor told Fay and Dick that there was nothing they could do for Michael. He said to take him home and wait for him to die. Really, that is exactly what the doctor said. My mother hated this doctor for his heart-shattering bluntness.

Six weeks later, Michael Howard Duchin, three years and seven months old, was buried in the family cemetery plot in New Jersey.

Much of the following information I learned mostly from my mother many years after the fact. The previous information was provided to give greater context to the personalities and socioeconomic circumstances of the Bronx Duchins, for, as many say, and I believe to be true, we are shaped by our environment and the things that occur in our lives, as much as by our genetic makeup.

When my identical twin brother Michael died, both my parents were understandably devastated. However, my father, in his terrible grief, decided to try to erase Michael's memory by discarding all the tangible things that were Michael's. Also, he would never speak about Michael, at least not in my presence. Even in later years, when I was more aware of past events, and asked questions about Michael, my father would turn away and leave the room. We had home movies of Michael and me, which for many years my father refused to show. At one point, and I can't recall how old I was, I learned, probably from my mother, that my father had cut a piece of Michael's curly blonde hair from his head as he lay in his little casket.

Often, as an adult, I've thought about how difficult it must have been for my parents to lose the mirror image of me, and then to struggle to put their lives back together with me present every day as a constant, living reminder that the duplicate of me was forever gone. Though I do not remember ever hearing it from my parents, I wonder if they feared losing me in the same way that Michael died. After all, we were identical twins. Doesn't that mean that I would have the same genetic flaws as Michael, yet to emerge in some horrible replay of Michael's illness and rapid decline? As an adult I've thought about this very thing many times. My blood is normal, and I've only had a small skin cancer when I was 35, that was entirely removed, with no recurrence, at least not so far.

Today, the greatest regret of my life, apart from the recent loss of my sweet Susan, is that I do not have any conscious personal memories of my brother Michael. If it were even possible for a three-and-a-half-year old to have such personal recall, and then to carry it forward into adulthood, my father's efforts to erase the memory of Michael made it far less likely that such memories would remain alive.

It's something I've prayed about for a long time now, to have my own true memories of my twin brother. It would be such a special blessing to remember Michael in a personal way, rather than from stories told to me by others, and from the many photographs and home movies that are now among my most valuable possessions. Although pictures are one dimensional frozen images, they're far better than nothing at all. Thank God for the photographs and movies of Michael and me!

My father acted in a very selfish and thoughtless way by wiping out the physical evidence of Michael's presence in all our lives, and doing the same with emotional evidence as well by declaring Michael a never-to-discuss topic.

Did the effects on me ever enter my father's tortured, grieving heart and mind? This was my identical twin brother!

Michael and I lived almost literally as one. We shared the same crib. We were pushed in the same baby carriage, side-by-side, not in the manner we see children today, commonly in rolling devices where one child is behind the other, not side-by-side. We were bathed together, we were each other's closest friends and worst enemies. We were virtually never apart from conception in the womb to the day that Michael died and suddenly and mysteriously disappeared from my life forever.

How often did I ask about Michael after he was suddenly gone? What did my parents say in response to my questions? How did I react to seeing my parent's visible signs of suffering in grief? I remember someone, maybe it was my mother, maybe it was my aunt Elaine, telling me that my mother stayed at her mother's apartment for weeks after Michael died . . . she just couldn't walk into our apartment. Did I ever see my mother during this time of her absence? Who took care of me during this time when mommy wasn't home? Was I scared? Did I cry? Was I angry? Was I confused? How did I adapt to sleeping alone for the first time in my life? What did I do now during the day when I would have been constantly playing with Michael? Did my father take any time off from work to be with mom and me? So many questions that will now remain unanswered because all those people directly involved at the time of Michael's death, relatives and friends of my parents, and my parents themselves, are now gone.

Here is where the so-called "intersection" lies. The old grief for my brother Michael bubbled up into my consciousness as my new grief engulfed me. The magnitude of this second experience with grief, the death of my wife, is so many levels beyond what I likely experienced as a small child when Michael died. However, remembering afresh the loss of my twin brother, and its life-altering reality, brought me to an intersection where these two events to some degree combined, causing a deeper sadness. Now, following Susan's death, my circumstances, my feelings, my fears, my anger, my pain, have intersected with my parent's circumstances at the time that Michael died. The revelation is not one that gives me any relief from my grieving, but it does give me relief from my ignorance. Knowledge gives me a sense of control. It is a false sense of control, but right now, I'll take it.

One thing has become so much more clear to me: I now understand grief and its capacity to erode a person's emotional health and stability. I now have a clearer window into my father's terrible pain, and a more compassionate understanding of why he acted as he did, trying to erase physical and conscious memories of Michael.

What my father did was not rational. It was a desperate emotional attempt to diminish his agony. It was like closing your eyes during a horror movie to avoid the shock. Except in this case everything that was happening was real. Although my mother handled it differently, I'm sure that her anguish was every bit as raw and intense as my father's. Mom still needed to be a mom and still had a three and a half year old child to take care of. She was forced to adapt quickly to the reality of what had occurred. Mom was at home with me all day while dad was at work and away from the house most of the day, at least from Monday through Friday. He was able to physically escape from the horrendous reality of how their lives had permanently changed. Mom did not have any physical escape. She was one tough lady. She was one extraordinary, loving, and devoted mother.

I hated my father for a very long time when I came to know more fully how he had behaved when Michael died. I never had a close or warm relationship with my dad, and I'm sure that there was a cause-and-effect dynamic at work, because I was a constant reminder of the dead child he wanted to avoid thinking about. My dad became overprotective of me, an understandable reaction in retrospect of course, when you view the circumstances dispassionately. The flames of my anger toward him burned intensely for many years, driving me to eventually seek psychological counseling off and on for years. The counseling was helpful and cathartic, but certainly no magic pill. Greater understanding doesn't necessarily yield a change in attitude.

In 2004 I learned of my father's death while I was at lunch with some colleagues during a business retreat. My brother Edward, five years my junior, and who still lived near my parents while I was living with my family in California, phoned to tell me the news. Dad had been in the hospital when he died at age 93, until then in reasonably good health. He wasn't expected to die. He took his last breath while eating, which is comically ironic because he loved to eat. So, in the sense that the family's expectations were different, it was a sudden occurrence. I remember receiving the news with hardly any emotion and I returned to the lunch table to finish my meal. Perhaps I was embarrassed to show emotion in front of my colleagues, especially in a public setting. But, I don't think this is the case. Quite simply, I never really knew the man that I called dad. I still feel shame about how I reacted to the news of his death. I flew to New York for dad's funeral and shed no tears at all. A 'for hire' rabbi, whom none of the family knew, spoke at the graveside service at the Jewish cemetery where my father was buried, the same cemetery where my brother Michael and my grandparents were buried. Though we shared the same compact living quarters in our Bronx, New York, apartment for the first 21 years of my life, a man I hardly knew had died.

I now believe that I understand my father's behavior in a way that I likely could never understand it other than by having to face a similar terrible reality. Is this helpful to me? Well, I feel that I now have some greater peace in that compartment of my brain where great disappointment in my father will always reside, and this, I suppose, is a good thing.

An important question for me now is: Might my experience possibly help me to help others? How can I take my experience and use it for good in my relationships with my family and friends, and in a wider context, in our broken world? This question gives me a window of hope and some degree of excitement. So far I've not been given a clear course direction by 'The Great Navigator.' Therefore, I must conclude, based on my faith in Him, that the next intersection He is preparing me to reach is somewhere further on down the road.

Chapter 40

Edward

In September 1946, when I was five years old, my parents, Fay and Dick Duchin welcomed a baby boy into the world, Edward Allen Duchin. If you work the calendar in reverse, the implication is that Edward was conceived just nine months after their little boy Michael died. Perhaps Fay and Dick were trying to get pregnant even sooner than nine months after Michael's tragic death. Though I never had any conversation about this with my parents, or anyone else for that matter, this strikes me as a very courageous step for them to take. It would not at all surprise me if my parents, or any parents for that matter, who lived through the unthinkable loss of a child, would not want to have any more children, ever. Apparently they did.

At the time of Edward's arrival we were living in the one bedroom apartment in the Bronx. I would guess—I can't remember because I was five years old at the time—that baby Edward slept in a crib near my parent's bed. Later, my parents gave the apartment's one bedroom to Edward and me to share, and they slept on a sofa bed in the living room. They continued to do this until we moved to the two bedroom apartment some years later.

Even after moving into the larger apartment, my brother and I shared a bedroom until I was 22 and got married. So for 17 years Edward and I bunked together.

Edward, 4 and Bobby, 9

It was clear from the start that Ed and I were very different people. Physically, we did not have a strong resemblance to each other, though certain subtle similarities were apparent to a careful eye. He was a very cute little guy, even with his ears that stuck out. Our personalities were worlds apart and our giftings were also very different. My earliest clear memory of one of our differences is when I was ten and Ed was five. By this time I was spending a lot of my time engaged in sports, primarily stickball and softball, in the schoolyard across the street from our building or in the nearby Bronx Park. My mom thought it would be enriching for me to learn to play the piano. So, my parents bought a used upright piano, found a piano teacher, Miss Selma Bleisch, and my piano lessons began. I enjoyed music and worked at my lessons, practicing every day in preparation for Miss Bleisch's weekly visit and critique. I think the lessons cost $5.00 for an hour, which at the time was no insignificant amount for my parents.

I remember that somewhere along the line, certainly less than a year after my piano lessons began, my little brother Ed, would come into the living room and sit quietly watching and listening as I stumbled through my weekly lessons. One day, after my lesson was finished, my five year old little brother went to the piano, hiked himself onto the piano bench, and played my lesson! We were all flabbergasted. Following this humiliation, I soon gave up the piano to devote more time again to playing ball, something that I was better at than Ed was.

Ed then began music lessons and progressed very rapidly. He was clearly very gifted musically. We discovered at some point that he had perfect pitch so that he could identify any musical note just by hearing it. I remember putting his gift to use in a sports context. Check this out. I was shopping for a tennis racket, my first one. I'd been told that the tighter the racket was strung, the better it was. So, I went with my brother to sort through the off-the-shelf rackets in the store. Striking a racket's webbing against the heel of the hand produced a sound, which was a musical note. Ed was easily able to tell me which racket was strung the tightest by listening to the pitch of the pinging sound made by the racket's strings. I then bought an E flat tennis racket, the tightest strung of the bunch that we tested.

Though we shared a room we did not get along well. Or, maybe we didn't get along well because we shared a room? Or, maybe I subconsciously resented Ed for taking Michael's place, the mirror-image 'roommate' who so mysteriously disappeared one day? Who knows. The result was still the same: We didn't get along. Sure, brothers tangle, often especially when they're youngsters, but I believe that we clashed more because we were wired so differently.

Another illustration of the differences between brothers is related to the use of dad's car when Ed and I were old enough to drive. Dad had to have his car every day for business, and we had only one car. If the car became disabled, let's say hypothetically, by teenage driver stupidity, dad could not work. Dad permitted us to use the car occasionally, but sometimes he would withhold use of the car as a penalty for something or another. Though this was disappointing to me, it wasn't the worst thing in the world to be deprived of the use of his business vehicle for a few days here and there. I dutifully accepted this judgment when it affected me. Ed, not so much. He secretly had keys to dad's garage made and would sneak the use of the car when he chose to, obviously for short periods of time, and on the weekends or evenings, when he was confident that dad would not need the use of the car. So the little brother who thought nothing of stabbing me (more on this ahead) had now grown into a car thief. No doubt he was fated for a life of crime.

Ed inherited musical talent that ran in the veins of some of the Duchins. A famous musician and orchestra leader in the 1940s was Eddie Duchin, a cousin of ours, who had a very distinctive style, and became a popular society orchestra leader in New York City. Eddie Duchin married a New York socialite. Apart from his talent, his connections with the rich and famous did him no harm. Sadly, Eddie Duchin's wife died in childbirth, then Eddie died of leukemia in the flower of life in 1951, leaving his only child, Peter Duchin, parentless, but not without means. Peter was raised until adulthood by the Harriman family, William Averell Harriman being a very prominent person. If 'Harriman' does't ring any bells for you, here's a bit of history.

Averell, as he was known, was the son of Edward Henry Harriman, (1848-1909), an American railroad executive. E. H. Harriman secured control not only of the Southern Pacific RR but also of the Central Pacific RR. Harriman used the financial strength of his railroads to buy widely and speculatively in railroad stocks elsewhere. He conducted the Harriman Alaskan expedition of 1899, a scientific undertaking; sponsored boys' clubs; and pledged $1 million and 10,000 acres of forest land to New York State for park purposes. The reservation, now the 42,500-acre Harriman State Park, is part of the Palisades Interstate Park.

William Averell Harriman expanded his railroad inheritance, became a banker and shipbuilder, and later became board chairman of the Union Pacific RR. He held many other positions of prominence including ambassador to the USSR and to Great Britain, U.S. Secretary of Commerce, governor of New York, and was an unsuccessful candidate for the Democratic presidential nomination in 1956. In 1968, when the Paris peace talks on the Vietnam War opened, he was chief U.S. negotiator. He is the author of Peace with Russia and America and Russia in a Changing World.

The Duchin name and the Harriman connection launched Peter Duchin's career as a spin-off of his father's success as a piano player and band leader amongst the society elite of New York City.

My brother Eddy, Eddie Duchin, and Peter Duchin all share a wonderful musical gift. Though Peter undoubtedly grew up in a highly privileged environment, I wonder if he would have traded it to have his parents around into their 90s as Ed and I were blessed to have?

History lesson over.

Though the older brother usually gets the best of the younger, especially in physical advantages, I remember one time that I was teasing my brother Ed to the point of distraction (I honed the skill of teasing to a truly fine art as I grew older), and I think that I was also knocking him around a bit. In frustration, Ed picked up a lead pencil and stabbed me in the knee. I was shocked and I let go of him immediately, screaming for mom and yelling at Ed, who I then believed had become a psychopath. The wound was minor compared with the surprise of it. I still bear a small, gray colored dot on my knee, stained by the lead tip of the pencil. You've heard "The pen is mightier than the sword." In this case, the number 2 pencil was mightier than big brother.

If I'd been my parents, I think I would have been relieved that Ed was so different from his older brother Bobby, thereby avoiding a physical connection to the twins and all the sadness this might dredge up once again. This is just my opinion; I have no facts in this regard to hang my hat on.

Though Ed made leaps and bounds of progress with his natural musical talent, soon outgrowing our piano teacher, Miss Bleisch, and performing in a recital or two, he decided early on that he did not want to be a performer; he wanted to play for personal enjoyment. I remember that he struggled academically in his first year of college, unsure of what he wanted to do with his life. His love for music didn't diminish and he played regularly at home on the Sohmer baby grand piano that our parents bought for him.

I had begun my career in Human Resources and at the time, in the 1960s, the "Kuder Preference Test" was a very popular instrument used to help people discover, or rediscover, their natural talents and preferences. Thus, it really wasn't a 'test', because there were no right or wrong answers. It was more a tool to mirror a person's interests and to then link these interests with possible occupations that would be compatible.

After seeing my brother struggling I suggested that he take the Kuder Preference Test. He agreed to do it. I brought home a copy and Ed took the test in our room at home. Not surprisingly to me, but I recall that it surprised him, his preferences were weighted very heavily in the direction of his natural gift, music. Soon after this, he dropped out of the college that he was attending and enrolled in a baccalaureate program at The Manhattan School of Music, where he had taken advanced music lessons for some time. His lessons there involved no small sacrifice for my parents in money and time. The school was in

Manhattan, not at all near our home, and my father would faithfully drive Ed to his lessons, wait for him, and then drive home.

The Manhattan School of Music is one of the finest institutions of its kind, offering bachelor's, master's and doctoral study programs in many music venues. The faculty is made up of members of New York City's leading performing institutions—the New York Philharmonic, Metropolitan Opera, New York City Opera, Chamber Music Society of Lincoln Center, Lincoln Center Jazz Orchestra, and the Orpheus Chamber Orchestra—as well as acclaimed individual artists. The school puts on 700 performances a year, including fully staged operas, orchestral concerts, and student and faculty recitals. Ed thrived and graduated with his bachelor's degree, choosing a career as a music teacher in the New York City public school system where he remained until he retired. While teaching he also succeeded in earning his master's degree in music theory from The Manhattan School of Music.

After I left my shared room with Ed to marry Susan, our relationship as brothers gradually changed. I must say that sharing a bedroom with Susan was considerably more enjoyable than sharing a bedroom with my little brother! Some of the change in our chemistry was to be expected as we grew older and matured into men pursuing their hopes and dreams without having to be in each other's faces every day and night. Ed continued to live at home for a while, then took his own apartment near our parents, until he married his wife, Marilynn, in 1974. By that time Susan and I had been married for 11 years, had three children, and were living in St. Louis, Missouri.

When Susan and I, or when I sometimes travelled alone to New York to see my family, we stayed at my brother's house, in Rockland County, just north of New York City. Though these visits were infrequent because of the distance and expense, I believe that they enriched our relationship. Ed also visited us in St. Louis a couple of times with his wife and daughter, Lauren. Lauren, now recently married, had her first child, Ella Reece, on my birthday in July. Ed is thoroughly thrilled to finally be a grandpa. With five grandkids on my scoreboard, here's another thing that I'm better at.

When dad died Ed felt the weight of it very heavily, while I did not. Ed had a much different relationship with dad than I did, I think largely because of dad's commitment to Ed's musical pursuits, dad driving him to his lessons, and the quality time thus logged between them.

Mom died a few years after dad passed away, and because of my closeness to my mother, her death hit me very hard. Mom was the most wonderful mother that I could have ever hoped for. She was a role model for so much of what became the core values of my life.

With both parents gone my relationship with my brother spiked in a positive direction. We come from a small family and with mom and dad gone, dad's only sibling gone, mom's two siblings gone, all four grandparents gone, Ed and I are the only remaining members of our immediate family. This cold fact motivated us to begin to draw closer by communicating more often and more meaningfully. We're still geographically distant from each other, Ed on the east coast, and me on the west coast. But we speak with each other regularly and our conversations are more intimate, and more meaningful, especially since Susan died. Ed knew Susan from the time she and I began dating. She loved my brother and he loved her. When Susan would come to my house to visit, Ed would play piano for her and she'd turn the pages of the sheet music and sing show tunes. They had a special relationship.

Ed's marriage ended in divorce after 27 years. He is now retired and living in Florida. For us it's still east coast versus west coast, yet we're both in places that are not likely to have snow in the winter. You don't have to shovel rain. I look forward to my phone conversations with my little brother.

Chapter 41

New Friendships

Susan and I were greatly blessed after settling into our retirement community where we quickly found wonderful new friends. The community is a self-contained development for folks 55 or older. It is gated, and has amenities including a beautiful 22,000 square foot clubhouse containing a banquet room and entertainment center, fitness center, media room where movies can be watched or borrowed, a library with computers for those that don't have one at home, a billiard room, recreation and meeting rooms, swimming pool, tennis courts, horseshoe pits, Bocce ball field, and shuffleboard court. There are many regularly scheduled activities available ranging from art classes to travel clubs.

We moved into our new home on a small cul-de-sac that includes eight houses. We soon discovered all our neighbors to be warm and friendly people. It just so happened that the couple who live right next door, Mike and Diana Stiles, are Christians who were leading a well-established Bible study made up of other residents in our community. We joined the group and have been meeting with them regularly for several years. This provided Susan and me with an accelerated connection with like-minded people who became friends and a close support group.

Susan and I especially connected with Mike and Diana. We'd been married about the same number of years, both couples had three children, and many life experiences turned out to be similar. It was always fun being together and sharing as we got to know each other more intimately. When the Stiles had friends over to their home they often invited Susan and me to join them and get to know their friends as our friends as we talked about life and laughed ourselves silly playing fun card games.

Susan and Diana became very close. We'd not had close friends like this for many years and I was especially happy for Susan who last had a best friend when we lived in St. Louis, Missouri, 27 years earlier! Mike and I have a strong connection as well though he still works full-time and therefore we don't have the time available to hang out as much as Susan and Diana did. Mike is also an avid golfer (his business is selling golf clothing), therefore he often spends his leisure time on a golf course. I'm not a golfer which eliminates that channel of further connection for us.

When Susan died I was deeply troubled by the thought that my relationship with Mike and Diana would diminish, my being a widower living alone, and them being a couple. My fears were soon squelched by Mike and Diana who, after I expressed my fear to them, assured me that our friendship would remain strong and that they would keep an eye on me. This has joyfully proven to be true. The Stiles have me over for meals, bring me goodies, and invite me to many of their family gatherings. They have become extended family and openly declare their love for me which is deeply touching. It isn't often that a man hears another man say "I love you", and mean it as a brother to a brother. I know how much more difficult it would be for me after losing Susan if I did not have the Stiles in my life. I regularly thank God for them. It was no accident that Susan and I settled in Menifee, California, within the housing development that we chose, and bought a home right next door to the couple that would become our closest friends.

There are other developing friendships that I hope will become deeper even though Susan is no longer part of the equation. Everyone loved Susan on contact. She just exuded an aura that generated a desire to be with her; no pretenses, no guile, just sweet Susan. She had an extraordinary warmth about her and a servant's heart. I'm a bit more complicated and do not make new friends as easily. I've always felt that having just a few good friends is blessing enough. I become extremely skeptical when I hear people talk about how many good or close friends they have. To me, "friend" means a lot more than acquaintanceship. It means someone you can confide in with complete trust, and someone who you can count on to help you in a pinch with anything you need. For example, when the Stiles are away from home, they give me the keys to their home and mailbox to get their mail, keep an eye on things, and water their plants. Susan and I did the same with them when we were away. This simple act is more than being a good neighbor. It is evidence of deep trust.

Since Susan died I've reconnected with some people who had been very special in our lives, but whom we had little or no contact with for many years. One extraordinary couple are Ron and Karen Lucas, who I write about in another section of this book. They were our best friends when we lived in St. Louis, Missouri. When I contacted them to tell them about Susan, it marked 25 years since we lived near one another. I believe that I'd not spoken with Ron in all that time, while Karen and her oldest daughter Jennifer, visited us once when we were living in Santa Barbara. Susan and Karen spoke on the phone a few times since the visit, but that was it. Reconnecting with them was as though no time at all had passed, because there was such a strong love between us as friends. They live in Texas, and have a home in Wyoming near their daughters, where Ron and Karen spend a good deal of their time. I hope that I will be able to see them sometime soon.

Another special reconnection is with my best friend from my college days at NYU, Steve Walsey. Steve and I pledged the same fraternity together and developed a strong bond of friendship. We attended each other's weddings and remained friends until Susan and I left New York City to live in New England. I often thought about Steve over the years but had not seen or had any contact with him for nearly 50 years when we reconnected by email and then by phone after Susan died. We now email regularly and speak on the phone from time-to-time. I hope to be able to see Steve face-to-face sometime soon. He lives and works in New York City.

The rekindling of these precious friendships has been a wonderful blessing, especially during my season of grieving. With Steve, as with Ron and Karen, it's as though we were never unconnected. Funny how that can happen with certain special people.

There are other friends from the various places Susan and I have lived over the course of my career that I've made a point to stay in contact with. These are wonderful friends too, and it is heartwarming that they wish to keep in touch. Yet there are always an extra-special few who will stand out above the rest because of common interests, unique experiences together, and many intangibles that I can only sum up as "strong chemistry".

When we left our birthplace, New York City, and embarked on our own as a young married couple, Susan and I made some wonderful friends while living in the Boston area for five years. At work I had a best friend, Curt Martha, without whom the lunacy of our workplace would have eventually ground me up and spit me out. We had a lot of outrageous, self-made fun with each other and with those around us. There was our exceptional HR office staff, Lucy Coco, Maureen Bulger, Carol Clarke and Peggy Wyndle. These young women still are among the finest people I've ever been blessed to know. There was the company's Controller, John Deneen, with whom Curt and I had extraordinary fun writing and saying outrageous things to each other that in today's workplaces would be grounds for disciplinary action or termination. There was Gayton Masters, Director of Marketing, and his lovely wife Rosemary, who remain extra-special friends, and Carol Reardon, a secretary in another department who was Curt's romantic interest. These are some of the marvelous people whom I miss and will never forget.

When we lived in the Santa Barbara area we helped to start a home group made up of a dozen or so people from our church. Three couples rotated the hosting and leading of the group gatherings every week; Randy and Dana Vandermey, Forest and Priscilla Mori, and ourselves. Finer people you would be very challenged to discover, let alone claim as friends. We decided at the outset that we wanted the group to be cross-generational, modeled after the early Christian church that met in peoples' homes because there were no church buildings and many were hostile to these followers of Jesus' teachings. We started each meeting with a simple meal together, then we'd gather for prayer and Bible study. We also wanted children to be welcome so that those with young children would not be inhibited from participating due to the cost of paying a babysitter. So, kids were part of our times together and typically the youngest of them were kept occupied by a member of our group who volunteered to spend time with them in another part of the house.

The dear folks in our home group were extended family and we got to know each other very well, evolving into a strong support group for one another. We met for a few years and I believe that we all benefited greatly from this special fellowship as we practiced loving one another, warts and all, trying to keep our focus centered on Jesus and His example. We didn't always succeed yet we knew the compass point that we had to try to keep steering toward.

Susan and I had other wonderful friends as we moved around the country. In retrospect I've often wondered how much more rewarding, in terms of developing even deeper friendships, it might have been if we'd planted our roots more firmly in one place. These were my choices as the head of my family. Although, if Susan had objected strongly I might have decided otherwise. But she did not. I now regret some of these choices. As the saying goes: You can't unscramble the egg.

I think about Frank and Sandy Kampschroeder, who were neighbors and dear friends in St. Louis. And Tom and Marlene Simpson. Tom, Ron Lucas and I would go out into the boonies in the winter to cut down trees for firewood. Tom had a wood burning furnace in his home and used the wood to heat his entire house. I used my share of the wood to simply enjoy our fireplace, although on a few occasions, due to power outages, we slept in our family room with only the warmth from our fireplace to keep us comfortable.

Jack and Maryann Muehlberger, another neighbor family we were close with in St. Louis. My boys and their boys were good friends and my oldest son still communicates with their oldest son from time to time. Larry and Susie Graveel, other neighbors in St. Louis. Larry worked for the same company I worked for. Though they were a generation younger than us, we became friends. Gary Bartick, with whom I connected in a men's Bible study group in Santa Barbara, at the time he was going through a divorce. It surprised and honored me deeply that Gary asked me to be his best man at his wedding when he remarried. Dan Drown, another men's group connection. Dan and I have kept in contact over the years, mostly by phone because he travels extensively. Dan was going through a very contentious divorce early in our friendship. I live vicariously through his travel experiences and it is very special to see him, though much more infrequently than I'd like. He remarried a few years ago to a delightful woman.

There were others too. Would these friendships have deepened and enriched all our lives even more had the Duchins not picked up and moved? I think it is more likely than not that at least some of them would have. Such is life. We live with, and hopefully learn from, the choices we make that cannot be changed. Maybe, when again confronted with similar circumstances, we'll make a better choice. I think that this is called wisdom.

Here are some thoughts about friendship attributed to some who have the gift of expressing in few words the essence of what I cannot even begin to express with many words.

> *"Friendship is unnecessary, like philosophy, like art . . . It has no survival value; rather is one of those things that give value to survival."*
> C. S. Lewis

"The happiest moments my heart knows are those in which it is pouring forth its affections to a few esteemed characters."
Thomas Jefferson

"This communicating of a man's self to his friend works two contrary effects; for it redoubleth joy, and cutteth griefs in half."
Francis Bacon

"The friendship that can cease has never been real."
Saint Jerome

"A friend is one to whom one may pour out all the contents of one's heart, chaff and grain together, knowing that the gentlest of hands will take and sift it, keep what is worth keeping and with a breath of kindness blow the rest away."
Arabian Proverb

"It is not so much our friends' help that helps us as the confident knowledge that they will help us."
Epicurus

"Walking with a friend in the dark is better than walking alone in the light."
Helen Keller

"Friendship that flows from the heart cannot be frozen by adversity, as the water that flows from the spring cannot congeal in winter."
James Fenimore Cooper

Chapter 42

Suralaya

I wrote the following barely two weeks after Susan died. My heart was in pieces and I cried and groaned with pain several times each day. It was my first written testimony about her, and at the time, I was so deeply grieved that I could not even write her name without breaking down with uncontrollable sobbing.

It occurred to me that an allegorical approach might enable me to use the bleeding ink from my heart in a way that would carry me into writing Our Story. The Bible is a great comfort to me, and my spirit gave to my consciousness the idea of writing in a biblical style.

And so I did, using Susan's Hebrew name, Suralaya, and mine, Baruch.

The Book of My Beloved

Suralaya 1

Recorded by Baruch, follower of the Lord Jesus Christ, who dwelt in the abundant and beautiful land of California, with many believing brothers and sisters.

A time of darkness has arrived for Baruch. Suralaya, his beloved wife of many years and his yokemate in Christ, is seriously ill once again after a respite of nearly three years.

A sudden emergency of breathlessness has placed a weakened and frightened Suralaya into the hands of the wise physicians.

Her heart is racing at a dangerously high level. She is so afraid of what is happening.

Over the next days Suralaya endures several surgeries to relieve life threatening conditions. Her heart and one lung are being crushed by fluid buildup. The procedures relieve the fluid but the trauma further weakens her.

One of the procedures confirms the worst fear: Suralaya's cancer has returned.

Suddenly, Baruch and Suralaya face prospects that lay a great heaviness upon them which would be so much more burdensome if not for the love of their dear Lord Jesus who helps them to carry this load that now grows more burdensome each passing day.

Those who know Suralaya, wife of Baruch, know full well the extraordinary sweetness, humbleness, and gentleness of her heart and spirit. She is loved by many.

She delights in preparing delectable offerings for her brothers and sisters. Willingly and joyfully Suralaya extends herself because she possesses a wonderfully giving heart and a great love and desire to serve others.

For Baruch, Suralaya's spirit is undoubtedly the sweetest of any person he has ever known. Baruch counts himself so greatly blessed to have her as his wife.

Suralaya 2

Suralaya poured herself into the upbringing of her children with an immeasurable depth of love and devotion. Her children are akin to the most special of special delicacies she could ever create. And she loves them unconditionally, deeply and unfailingly.

She takes a special joy in her five grandchildren whom she loves as she loves her own children.

She has always been long-suffering of Baruch's far different and often irksome behaviors because her promised love for him was a lifelong commitment before God, God's people, and even unto the unbelieving. To Baruch she gives her love fully, unconditionally, and unfailingly.

There are people who seem as though they have been born with a greater capacity for unconditional love, forgiveness of hurts, and for joyfully giving to others. Suralaya is one of these rare people who thus so richly blesses others.

Thus, Baruch knows the wondrous blessing that God has given him through his dear wife, Suralaya, but he deeply regrets that he has not often enough expressed to Suralaya how deeply he loves and appreciates her; how special to him she truly is.

What the future may hold is not clear at this time. The imagined worst prospects of what the Lord God may permit are both mind-numbing and terrifying at the weakest of moments. But these moments have been remarkably, unexplainably few. Most of the time thus far, the peace of God that is beyond Baruch's grasp reigns in his heart and mind.

How great and loving is our Father God and our Lord Jesus Christ!

The outpouring of love, prayer, and offers of help from brothers and sisters who are nearby, other brothers and sisters scattered in more distant places, and friends who may not know Jesus as their Lord and Savior, is overwhelming, and so precious a gift to Baruch and Suralaya at this trying time.

How do those who do not know Jesus Christ as their personal Savior, who have not the confidence of the promised eternal life after death, in a perfect Heaven, journey through dark seasons like this?

There is much that Baruch cannot comprehend of the mind of God whose thoughts are so much higher than any mortal's thoughts could ever be.

Baruch dwells on God's love, God's Word, God's perfection, and God's utter reliability, and clings to Scripture of great promise such as the nearly unbelievable statement by the Lord Jesus Christ—though Baruch does truly believe it—found in John 15:9: "Just as the Father has loved Me, I have also loved you; abide in My love."

And so, in the midst of this time of darkness and trepidation, Baruch and Suralaya are trying to find a place of refuge under the protection of God's mercy and grace, knowing that He ultimately desires only good for His children, and that His purposes cannot be thwarted by anyone or anything in Heaven or on Earth.

To Him is the Kingdom and the Power and the Glory now and forever!

Suralaya 3

Suralaya has not regained her strength for which so many have prayed and hoped. She is languishing, coughing fitfully and often. She has difficulty breathing, and she is weaker and more tired. The wise physicians are not sure why this is happening following the life-saving procedures that were performed.

Terrible fear grips Baruch's heart. He is deeply troubled. Before Baruch's very eyes Suralaya diminishes in strength.

Fits of sudden anger overcome Baruch, as well as waves of heavy sadness. Back and forth these consuming emotions rebound off each other bringing great frustration and confusion, along with exhausting stress.

Baruch knows that he has no control whatsoever over what he is experiencing. Only God can be implored to bring hope and mercy into these circumstances.

Suralaya barely takes nourishment and lies in bed with her eyes closed much of the day. Baruch ponders with great anxiety the discouraging and frightening signs that he cannot avoid watching.

The wise physicians regularly visit Suralaya and offer expressions of hopeful outcomes. Baruch clutches at these hopes yet somehow does not believe that he can rely on them.

Baruch prays constantly for God's touch of healing and comfort for his beloved, and he knows that so many others are doing the same on her behalf. How comforted they both are knowing that many dear ones are holding them up in prayer.

Day and night Baruch prays and cares for his beloved Suralaya. He brings her food that she requests only to see her barely eat any. She drinks little fluid. She is losing weight. She can walk only a short distance without tiring. She is not improving.

Suralaya 4

Yet a second emergency of breathlessness while at home takes Suralaya back into the care of the wise physicians. She has now been declining for weeks.

Baruch waits for the physicians to help her, praying unceasingly to the Great and Mighty God and His beloved Son, Jesus.

The physicians perform many examinations as she passes a birthday in their care without the strength to even open celebratory letters from friends and loved ones.

Baruch's heart is clenched in pain. Watching his beloved Suralaya suffer is difficult beyond description. Baruch spends all day, each day, at Suralaya's bedside, praying and trying to provide her with comfort and protection.

The results of the wise physicians' examinations is dreadful news. Despair now becomes more intense.

On the very day of celebrating Suralaya's birth, the most learned of the wise physicians tells Baruch that there is no earthly prospect for healing.

The startling message is that Suralaya may not survive more than a matter of days! Baruch is thunderstruck and can taste bitter despair in his throat.

Baruch finds it unbelievable that his beloved Suralaya, so full of life until just recently, who brings so much joy to others, will very soon be departing the earthly shell that her sweet spirit inhabits.

Suralaya and Baruch have been wife and husband for 47 years. They have known each other for 54 years. Baruch finds it unimaginable to be without her.

They have looked forward with such pleasure to spending their sunset years taking care of each other and watching their beautiful grandchildren blossom. The thought of this being taken away is too terrible to ponder.

Baruch shakes with anxiety at the briefest thought of this happening. He requires medication to assist him in remaining reasonably functional and not to add to Suralaya's fears.

The most learned of the wise physicians speaks with Suralaya and Baruch together. He is kind and gentle with his words. The terrible conclusion that is now rapidly approaching is not stated explicitly, yet it is clearly understood. Suralaya cries mournfully.

Suralaya 5

With stunning and terrifying swiftness Suralaya becomes physically unresponsive. She is breathing with assistance but there is no physical movement.

Baruch and Suralaya's son, Adam, who has lovingly rushed to be at the side of his beloved mother and to support his father, try to bravely endure the horrible event unfolding before their eyes.

Suralaya's daughter, Andrea, who has traveled from a distant place, sadly arrives too late to converse with her beloved mother. With deep sorrow and regret she sees her dear, dear mother barely alive.

Baruch, his son, and his daughter, feel a kind of pain and emptiness that takes their breath away and numbs their sensibilities. But it is good that they can be together at this time.

The physicians who are watching over Suralaya now say that Suralaya has no more than a day left on earth! Oh dear God, this is such a horrifying message to hear!

Baruch is almost paralyzed with anguish. Why will this wonderful wife and mother be taken away so quickly?

To Baruch, 47 years married to his beloved now seems like not nearly enough time.

Baruch yearns to have more time to tell Suralaya how much he loves her and how he regrets any hurt he has ever caused her.

He wants so much to hold her in his arms again and have her respond with love and joy. He wants to take care of her and protect her. He wants to change this grotesque reality to a different, more hopeful one.

Baruch and Suralaya have not had the chance to say goodbye to one another, share a last tender kiss, a last embrace. This breaks Baruch's heart.

It is so overwhelmingly sad for Baruch who knows that he will remember this sudden ripping apart from his beloved until his own last day in this world.

Baruch feels a part of his own self dying.

Though Suralaya is unresponsive except for her breathing, the wise physicians say that she can hear what is being said. Baruch hopes that this is true; he needs for this to be true.

He needs her to hear his familiar voice so that he can try to comfort her pain and her fear. He needs Suralaya to hear him so that he can have some greater semblance of closure, though it will be so far less than he wants.

He speaks to her constantly. While she barely lingers in life he wants her to know that he is right there with her.

She appears peaceful yet it is extremely disturbing to Baruch that her eyes are barely open and not blinking. The physicians assure Baruch that she is not in pain and Baruch is so deeply thankful to his great and wondrous Lord and Savior, Jesus Christ, that this is so.

Though Baruch desperately wants to have just one more conversation with his beloved Suralaya, it is not to be.

Baruch promises Suralaya that he will not leave her side until the very end. He continues to hold onto the belief that she truly can hear his voice. The impending outcome is almost unbearable for Baruch to think about but he will not leave her side.

Baruch sits at Suralaya's bedside watching her beautiful, still face, with just slivers of her lovely blue eyes showing. He often has told her that she has beautiful eyes. He continues his bedside vigil through the rest of the day and all through the long night.

Suralaya's daughter will be returning to her home and so Baruch's son and daughter leave to try to get some rest before the son must awaken early the next morning to transport his sister to her place of departure.

Suralaya 6

The night passes with interminable slowness with Baruch alone at his beloved's side drawing himself as close to her bed as possible and gently holding her hand.

It is as though everything in the world has stopped except for the shallow breaths that Suralaya is taking, and Baruch watches this evidence of lingering life as though he were watching over the most valuable treasure on earth. It is now, truly, the most valuable treasure on earth to Baruch.

Baruch dozes fitfully at Suralaya's side, watching her breathing, staring into her beautiful face, telling her over and over again how much he loves her, kissing her face and hand, telling her how deeply he will miss her.

Baruch senses that Suralaya's heart is troubled, and so he tells her that if she believes that he has not forgiven her for anything that steals her peace, that she should know that everything and anything that may be adding weight to an already immensely overburdened spirit and soul, is completely forgiven.

Baruch is still praying and hoping for God to intervene with a miracle of healing.

But sweet Suralaya is so ill and weak that the good physicians who are watching over her say that the end is now very near. The incredibly long night passes for Baruch with little change in Suralaya's condition.

He remains at her side, holding her hand, whispering loving words to her, through the long night.

Baruch's son rejoins him at his mother's bedside early the following morning. Suralaya lies quietly before their eyes, still completely unresponsive.

Suralaya's barely open eyes present an eerie and disturbing contrast: This dear, deeply loved wife, mother and companion, only a few weeks ago was as vibrant as she had been most of her life.

The kind physicians administer a strong potion to Suralaya to ensure that any pain she may be feeling will quickly be blocked. Baruch believes that it is more for his and his son's comfort than Suralaya's, but he is very grateful.

Baruch regularly kisses Suralaya's face and gently strokes her cheeks and her soft hair.

Baruch continues to hold Suralaya's hand which is still warm with life. He recalls that she has always had such soft and smooth skin, and even at this moment she still does.

Perhaps she does not feel his touch but it is a great comfort for Baruch to hold her hand in his.

Baruch prays and begs for some response from her to show that she hears his expressions of love. He implores her to blink her eyes or to squeeze his hand in response to his voice. Sadly, sadly, sadly, there is no response of any kind from his dear Suralaya.

It is so crushing to Baruch's already deeply aching heart that not even the slightest responsiveness occurs.

A last intimate exchange between lifelong partners, even with the slightest animation on her part, would be so immensely comforting.

Suralaya is alive, but seemingly unaware of anything happening around her.

The heartache that Baruch is now feeling is intensely palpable to him, but no words could describe it. There is a terrible, painful knot in the center of Baruch's chest. This is a cruel dream. Please dear, merciful God, he prays, end this nightmare!

But no: It is not a dream. It is a heartbreaking and terrible reality.

Suralaya 7

The early morning hours drift ever so slowly forward. The waiting is torment.

Then Suralaya's breathing suddenly stops.

This instantly awakens Baruch's exhausted senses.

After a moment Suralaya takes a breath, and then again her breathing ceases. And this happens one more time after which no further breathing is discernible.

Baruch's son rushes to find the caregivers, who arrive quickly. They carefully seek signs of life, but find none.

Baruch lies across sweet Suralaya's quiet form. He kisses her lips and sobs uncontrollably, declaring through blinding tears his love for her and how much he already misses her.

One of the good physicians arrives and examines her. He pronounces her gone, and warmly expresses his condolences.

Baruch and his son are left alone for a time with the lifeless form of the wife and mother whose precious spirit has just passed from its prison of a damaged human body, to life eternal in Heaven, with a perfect new body.

Though Baruch knows that Suralaya no longer suffers, his human heart is already deeply aching with the onset of grief.

Baruch uncontrollably and without shame sobs for his sweet, sweet Suralaya, now gone from the trappings of her battered body, gone from this Earth, and gone from his life.

The heavy burden of grief that Baruch feels is more terrible than anything he has ever experienced. It is both frightening and debilitating. He shakes uncontrollably and has difficulty standing.

Yet it is so much more bearable for Baruch knowing that Suralaya will never suffer again. Baruch will be with his beloved again someday, though he must live out his appointed days in mortal time, while Suralaya now lives in utter joy in a timeless and eternal Heaven.

Chapter 43

Growing In Love

Falling in love. It was such a precious time in our lives for Susan and me. To me the expression "falling in love" is a strange one. It brings to mind a picture of an accident over which there is little or no control. I've fallen, literally, several times in recent years with resulting serious physical injuries and multiple corrective surgeries. In no way did I intend to fall. I had little or no control over these painful events.

So, I'd prefer to substitute 'growing in love', for 'falling in love.' I'm so glad now that, for us, it was a slow and evolving process. It made it last longer. It was like ice cream that barely melts so that you can take as long as you want to savor it with little discernible decrease in the amount of ice cream . . . as though it was magically replenishing itself as it is being enjoyed. And, the flavor is continuously evolving, becoming more and more delicious, as time goes by.

The feelings that energized this growing in love process were the most wonderful feelings that I imagine any human being could ever hope for. I know that so much more now than ever before. Then, I only loved being in it, caught up in it, which believe me, is not a declaration of disappointment. It's just a recognition that wisdom, insight, and fuller appreciation of the precious things in life and relationships, particularly growing in love with someone, fully develops only with the passage of time.

Chapter 44

Time Drifting

The sense of being transported back in time often emerges these days. Not dreaming while restlessly asleep during the terribly lonely nights that occur now every night. I mean clear imaginings during the bright daylight hours. At this very moment. The imaginings are vivid, and often joyful even through tears.

This takes my attention away from the disturbing pictures branded into my mind that I've continued to have, though I thank God that these awful mental pictures are diminishing now: of her body sliced and stitched by surgeons, enormous bruises and fresh scars that made me wince when I looked at them, terrible pain that she endured as she lay weakened and helpless in an ICU hospital bed. Tubes in her arms, down her throat, pumping vital fluids, strong drugs, and oxygen into her, and a large tube in her side, as well as a urinary catheter, drawing fluids out of her body, and Susan with not enough strength to get out of bed to use the toilet.

My time-drifting was not expected. Sure, I've had many days when I've thought about Susan when she was young and healthy. But I did not expect to feel as though we are together again, back in time, reliving our courtship. Yes, that's what's happening: I'm reliving our courtship! I'm growing in love with her all over again. Not that I ever grew out of love with her. What I mean is that as I look at old photos of both of us from the 1950s and 1960s, and read the 85 letters we exchanged before we were married, I'm reminded of how lovely she was, and how precious and rare was our tender, budding love.

What memories now bubble to the surface of my mind? So many warm memories compete in my mind now, and I'm struggling to put them in chronological order before writing them down. But that's plain ridiculous isn't it! I can reorder them to my heart's content any time I want. Right now I must capture them while they're fresh. So I'm going to try to just let things pour out of my heart in whatever order they occur. I'll fiddle with organizing it some other time—or maybe not at all.

So, here's another question, one that I'm almost afraid to ask. Is it a sign of mental or emotional instability to be growing in love with my dead wife?

It seems at the least very peculiar to me. Yet, I'm not fighting the compelling urges because it's helping to validate that my love for her was so deep and so very real. This is very important to me right now as I continue to have bouts of guilt. Guilt over feeling that I did not love her enough, or that I didn't love her unconditionally, or that I was too hard on her by stubbornly holding onto expectations that she resisted over many years of our marriage. Or maybe I'm afraid that I will forget her . . . this is a truly terrifying thought!

It also gives me pleasure to remember those times in our lives when so much future was spread out in front of us, and we were enveloped with so much hope and excitement for that future together. Finding pleasure these days is a very challenging thing for me. So I'm hungrily ingesting and savoring the pleasure I find in my time drifting. I hope that it turns out to be a contribution to my healing rather than a detriment. I just don't know right now where it will take me.

Love matures. It ages. It becomes more complex with the passage of time, like fine wines. Like the development of fine wines, fine love requires careful cultivation and patience. This aging process renders it different. The maturing of love happens in indistinct stages that often overlap thus making the stages even more indistinct so that you don't fully know it's happening until sometime later on when you stop and look back. Then you notice in retrospect, and perhaps even marvel at the fact that chapters of life-irretrievable have been written in the wake of regular, everyday living.

The metamorphosis of growing love became the most wonderful gift for Susan and me so early in our lives, to find each other, and to become the love of each other's lives, until death would part us.

Along with the old photographs that I've rediscovered, I came across a needlepoint that Susan made for me many years ago; she loved to do needlepoint. It says:

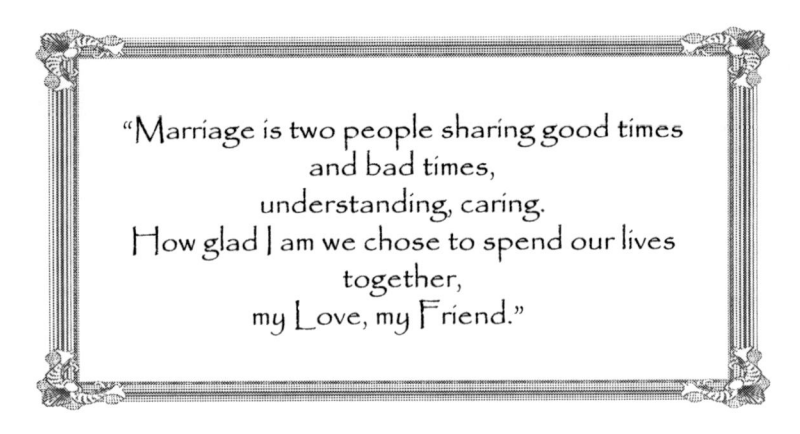

> "Marriage is two people sharing good times
> and bad times,
> understanding, caring.
> How glad I am we chose to spend our lives
> together,
> my Love, my Friend."

I framed this beautiful and tender remembrance. It's on display in our home where I can now see it every day.

Chapter 45

Old Photographs

I watched a movie recently that triggered some memories about our wedding photos. The male star of the movie is an amateur photographer who is asked to take some black and white photos at an upcoming Bar Mitzvah celebration because the boy's mother liked black and whites for their "artistic" quality.

Susan and I chose to have a black and white photo album of our wedding, though I really don't remember exactly why. I don't think 'artsy' would have accurately described either of us. Maybe my parents got a special deal and everyone knows that Jews can't resist special deals . . . wink, wink.

That's correct, I said "my parents." Traditionally the bride's parents pay for the wedding, right? At least that was the tradition in our generation. Susan's parents claimed that they did not have the money at the time and said that if my parents paid for the wedding, they would repay my parents later. It never happened. My parents never brought it up to them. This 'transaction' revealed a difference in family character that proved to be an omen of much more serious issues, yet to be revealed.

I've been looking through our wedding pictures and many other old photos these days and the visual stimulation resurrects many memories that have been lying dormant in some of my rapidly aging brain cells. I'm grateful for the wake up call.

After pouring through four large cartons of old photos and 35 mm color slides, I've done something I've been meaning to do for many years now: sort them. Now I've got a stack of plastic bins labeled for each of my children, my brother, Susan's brother, and so on. Next step: to go back through the bins and cherry-pick the photos that I want to keep, and then pass on to my children and other relatives the remainder, which will be many pictures.

I know how much I cherish photos of my parents, grandparents, aunts and uncles, cousins, and friends, most of whom are now deceased. I hope that my children will cherish these photos plus the ones that Susan and I added, and that they will show them to their children, telling them about the people in the photos. Perhaps someday this younger generation will hand them down to their children to continue a family legacy of remembrance.

I was determined to find all the pictures of Susan and me that I could. Mission accomplished! I did not clearly remember how beautiful Susan was in her late teens, twenties and thirties, in the 1950s, 60s, and 70s. Not that she wasn't beautiful after those periods of time; you know what I mean. The youthful beauty that eventually and inevitably morphs due to age, genetics, lifestyle, metabolism, and gravity, is a one-time deal.

Its been a pleasure and, believe it or not, a sensual stimulation, to 'see' her again at the peak of her youthful, natural beauty. Her big blue eyes, the sprinkling of freckles across the bridge of her nose, her full, pouty lips, graceful neck, and lovely figure. I chose a dozen or so of my favorite photos of her and had them digitized and cleaned up a bit by a local photo studio. No airbrushing of her natural loveliness, just some cleanup of distracting things like scratches and specks, and the removal of irrelevant things like wall hangings and furniture that cluttered the pictures. I'm planning to frame some of them.

Susan and Bob 1961

Chapter 46

A Terrible Secret Revealed

Some years after we were married and started our family, Susan and her parents became estranged and remained so for the rest of our married lives because of tragic circumstances that had a severe impact on Susan between the ages of 14 and 16. These circumstances caused deep emotional wounds that lasted her entire life and brought about many trying times in our marriage.

What I'm about to share was disclosed to me by Susan before we were married. She was 18 or 19 at the time. We may have already been engaged to be married . . . I'm not sure, but it was close to that time. It did not come out easily because I think that she was not only ashamed, she may have also thought that I would not love her or not want to marry her after I learned of it. I don't remember what triggered the conversation. I admired her greatly for her courage and willingness to be so vulnerable. This is a testament to her character and to her trust in me. It tested our love for each other.

Susan told me, just a few years ago, that I am the only man she's known in her life whom she has trusted.

Just pause and think about this almost incredible statement and how its implications might affect the life of a woman, beginning when she was just an innocent young girl.

This extraordinary statement is the greatest compliment I've ever received in my life, and I am so deeply honored that I was able to earn Susan's trust and her love. But it caused me to be overwhelmingly sad for her.

Between the ages of 14 and 16, Susan, a completely sexually innocent, lovely teenage girl, under the protection of her parents in their home, was subjected to premeditated, methodical, and repeated criminal and predatory sexual abuse by her father.

I use the words "criminal" and "predatory" in a literal as well as in a legal context because these are the terms used in the text of the laws of the State of New York. By committing these acts her father was not only an unfit parent, he also was a despicable pervert, and a criminal. Under the laws of New York State, her father was guilty of no less than four felonies, and one misdemeanor. If he'd been charged, he might have said that it was consensual, though it was not. But this would be a nonstarter as a legal defense because under New York law, a person is deemed incapable of consent to sexual conduct if less than 17 years old.

These horrible molestations occurred in the middle of the night, in Susan's bedroom, in the apartment that Susan, her parents, and her two brothers shared. Her brothers were 12 and 17 at the time it began.

Susan's father would sneak into her room and violate her sexually. She told me that she had no idea at the time that this was unnatural and believed it was likely that her girlfriends were doing the same thing with their fathers. I suspect that her father fed her this fable.

I listened to this confession from the girl that I dearly loved, and cannot put into words how shocked, disgusted, and enraged I was—not with Susan, but with her father, and her mother! Her father, with premeditation, stole his own young daughter's innocence and inflicted a terrible scar on her psyche that would never completely heal. In view of the relatively small size of their apartment, and the proximity of the bedrooms, there is no doubt in my mind that Susan's mother consciously did not intervene.

Susan's father was an accomplished Deceiver. For two years he regularly sexually molested his daughter. He did this while acting as the responsible family provider, and the comedian at family gatherings, playing the piano, singing, doing card and cigarette tricks, and cavorting with their dog, Rusty, and other behaviors that I believe were all calculated to camouflage who and what he really was. Everybody liked Susan's father. Nobody really knew him, or if they did, it would add another layer of sickness and tragedy to this dark chapter of the Geller family's lives. Susan was always respectful to her parents. She was afraid of her father.

Ironically, Susan's father was a strict disciplinarian with his daughter, imposing a strict 10:00 pm curfew, instructing that she be her mother's helper for cleaning and cooking, and when Susan went to work after graduating high school, he insisted that she pay a portion of the rent, which she dutifully did. Susan was a Cinderella figure in her household.

It is unimaginable to me that a father could do something like this to his daughter. And to do it repeatedly over a two year period, in his own house, while the rest of the family was *supposedly* fast asleep offers a chilling picture of a very disturbed family.

Chapter 47

Some Things Can't Be Changed

From the moment Susan told me her terrible secret I hated her father with a fury that I've never felt toward another person, even to this day. As I later processed this information I came to also despise her mother because nothing in Heaven or Earth could ever convince me that over this two year reign of sexual terror under her mother's roof, that Susan's mother had no knowledge or even a suspicion of what was going on. Susan's mother, Rose, was the only possible line of defense for Susan in this horror story. I'm certain that Rose pretended as though it wasn't happening.

God only knows what was wrong in Louis and Rose Geller's marriage. Rose was not physically attractive, a mediocre cook, and often spent the day robed in what was then called a 'Muumuu', which was a plain, straight, long, house-dress. Her only apparent gift was a beautiful singing voice. No matter. The behavior of these parents was despicable and criminal. On many occasions I wavered in my mind between beating Louis to a pulp, or turning him in to the police, or both. I did neither because Susan begged me not to. We were not married yet and she was terrified of the consequences if I was to blow the cover off this nightmare while she was still living with her parents. If it had still been going on I would have done everything possible to see that Susan's father paid a steep price for his crimes.

From the point of learning from Susan about her being sexually abused by her father, as you might expect, my attitude toward her parents changed. Not outwardly, believe it or not. One of my strengths was, and still is, a very high degree of self-control. I can bury my emotions when I want to. This is not the healthiest of behaviors in the long run, but it got Susan and me through the period between my learning of the evil in her home, and the time that we would marry and I could physically rescue her from her parents. We could not wait for this to happen. In the meantime Susan did not want the boat rocked, and I honored her wishes.

Many years later, after a long period during which Susan was estranged from her parents, and during which time her brothers wanted to know from her why she was treating their parents coldly, Susan, for the first time, told her brothers what had been done to her as a young girl. They didn't believe her. At least not until her older brother, Robert, learned from his wife that Susan's father made advances toward her! Then, Susan's older brother believed it.

After our daughter Andrea was born and when Susan's parents visited us, which did not happen often, thank God—or when we visited them, also not often—we were very watchful of our daughter in the presence of Susan's father. We vowed to never permit Andrea to be alone with her grandfather, Louis. How disgustingly sad is that?

Twelve years into our marriage, and after Susan and I had become born-again Christians, Susan felt led by God to forgive her father for what he'd done to her. At this time her parents were retired and living in Florida, and we'd not seen them in a very long time. The sexual molestation by her father that Susan had endured for so long scarred her deeply. Her perception of her personal worth was doomed to be distorted, and it was. As you might imagine, it also seriously affected our marital intimacy. Suffice to state that it caused a dark cloud to always be not very far away as we worked to be husband and wife.

This is why I found it incredible that she would want to forgive the disgusting excuse for a father who had hurt her so profoundly. Not only did she decide to forgive him, but she wanted to travel to Florida to do so face-to-face! I raged and ranted about this plan of hers, warning that her father would only deny that anything ever happened and thereby create a new wound. I feared the reopening of deep wounds. She was adamant and would not be swayed.

Susan went to Florida, and sought and found a brief, opportune moment, as she told me about it later, to be alone with her father. She told him simply that she was led by God to forgive him for what he had done to her. His reaction was shock and tears, and he thanked her, never uttering even a syllable of denial. He begged her not to ever tell her mother. What a low life cowardly scum!

Susan never did say anything about it to her mother, from whom she became more and more distant over the years.

After we were married, Susan, having been raised as a dutiful Cinderella figure, was always the one to initiate phone contact with her mother and endure her mother's litany of complaints about her illnesses, real and imagined. Until one day, Susan just became fed up with her mother's selfish expectations and decided that she was not going to call her mother anymore until her mother initiated a call to her. For years I had been pleading with Susan to change the rules of this game between her and her mother. Following Susan's phone conversations with her mother, Susan was always disappointed. You know what? Her mother never called her. So their contact with one another simply ended. I must admit that I was thrilled imagining her mother's outrage that her daughter wouldn't call her anymore to check on her well-being. As it is said, what goes around comes around.

This was the mother that allowed her virgin daughter to be a sexual sacrifice to her perverted husband, right under her nose. And yes, I remain thoroughly convinced that she full well knew what was going on, and never lifted a finger to protect her precious, young, innocent daughter.

As hard as I've tried to forgive her father and her mother for what they did to Susan, I can still be easily thrown into a state of teeth-clenching anger when I think about the impact that these disgraceful parents had on their precious young daughter, and then on both Susan and me as husband and wife.

Susan claimed a victory that I'm not sure that I ever really will have, or quite honestly, that I ever really want. She found peace with her Heavenly Father first, then with herself, and then with her earthly father. This is an amazing testament to Susan's inner beauty and the strength of her faith in God!

I suppose that I'm unwilling to yield to God's promises that He will ultimately bring about justice for every person. Though I truly believe that God will do this, I've not been able or willing to let go of my hatred for her parents. This is not something that I'm proud of. I know it is not what God wants from me. It simply is what it is. God help me.

Chapter 48

Teen Dating In The 1950s

I walk about half a mile from home to the public bus stop on Pelham Parkway to catch the #12 bus west, pay the $0.15 cent fare, and soon ride past the main entrances to the world famous Bronx Zoo, and on the opposite side of the road, the beautiful New York Botanical Gardens, a virtual oasis in the heart of the Bronx. The bouncy, noisy, exhaust fume-spewing, large city bus cruises west down Fordham Road, past the Fordham University campus on the right, and on to where Fordham Road intersects with the Grand Concourse, a long, very wide, and very attractive boulevard lined with apartment buildings and scattered commercial establishments.

This ride, with many quick stops along the way to pick up and drop off passengers, takes about 20 minutes. I get off the bus in front of Alexander's Department Store, a famous hub of shopping activity for tens of thousands of Bronx shoppers in the 1950s and 1960s. I can then use a free transfer for another bus to head south on the Grand Concourse for about a mile. Or, I can walk, which I often have done, depending on the weather. My destination is a particular building, two blocks east of the Grand Concourse, less than a mile from Yankee Stadium to the south.

This building is where Susan Geller lives with her family. She is the love of my life. It's a Saturday, early evening, and I'm picking her up to go to a movie at the Loew's Paradise Theater, on the Grand Concourse, a 10 minute walk from her family's apartment.

The Loew's Paradise Theater was a magical place. It was one of those movie houses that was grandly and ornately designed so that it felt like you were entering a palace when you passed though its doors. A palace in the middle of the Bronx! When you walked from the lobby into the theater itself: another world entirely! It was a feast for the senses and a very romantic portal.

The theater's ceiling is concave and painted dark blue like an evening sky, and when the lights dim for the movie, the ceiling transforms into a night sky complete with faintly twinkling electric stars. Around both sides of the theater are faux balconies and painted murals, leaving the impression that you are outdoors, perhaps in an old town square somewhere, definitely not in the Bronx, New York. Many Bronx public schools held their graduation ceremonies at the Paradise Theater because of the setting and because it had a seating capacity that could accommodate the size of graduating classes that exceeded the schools' seating capacities. Two of my public school graduations, including high school, were held in this magnificent setting. So, for the price of two movie tickets, Susan and I were transported into another world for a short period of time.

Susan was 16 and I was going on 18 at this time. Teenagers still, but close to the cusp of adulthood, still under the authority of our parents in our respective parents' households, but not for very much longer.

The dimming of the lights in the magic of the Paradise Theater created an instant intimacy that we could not ever have enjoyed anywhere else at this time in our lives because the culture of the time weighed against it. We could never expect to be in such close physical proximity to each other in either of our family's households, in the dark, without parental surveillance, for two hours or more. I did not have much access to my father's car at this time. The intimacy of the two of us alone in a car was a heart-throbbing fantasy, but that's all it was, a fantasy.

So we'd sit side-by-side in the theater, holding hands, and finding it thrilling and intimate because we were touching each other, even in this benign and innocent way. Love between us was budding at this time and so this was more than just a night out for two teenagers. This was titillating to youngsters who were growing in love with each other. Of course there were hundreds of other people around us in the theater, and above us as well in the balcony. But they were all strangers and so they were as invisible to us as we were to them. We were in our own special world for the next two hours.

These were moments that I did not want to end except for one thing that contradicted this feeling. Though it would mean that we would be apart again until our next date, an interminable week away, I could barely wait to walk her home at the end of our date. Because this would mean that either in the shadow of the stairwell on the floor below her family's apartment, or at the door to the apartment, I would finally get to kiss her sweet lips and hold her close to me as we were saying goodbye. She would remove most of her lipstick so as not to smudge my mouth, and we would embrace with our mouths melting together in tender kisses. Her mouth was so sweet. Her lips were so warm and soft. We explored each other's tongues. We nibbled and kissed first tenderly and then harder. It was almost more than I could bear knowing that this would only last a minute or two, and that I would have to will the feelings to last until the next time, a distant week away.

She put her arms around my neck and I held her tightly, often pressing against her body with no resistance on her part. We would melt together, locked in delicious surrender to each other, and then, we had to stop. Susan had a curfew of 10:00 pm, and we often cut it close not wanting our time together to end. Sometimes her father would call from inside the apartment obviously having heard us just outside the door, breaking the magic spell of the most intimate and exciting moments of our deepening relationship.

Those sweet kisses were more than just two sets of lips pressed together in sensual pleasure, though it certainly was that as well. It was the tender beginning of a much more complex and meaningful joining of two hearts. It was as though each kiss, each moment together, every loving glance into each other's eyes, every smile, laugh, and giggle, even the arguments, were the beginning of a beautiful life-tapestry that our relationship began to weave.

> "How very lovable her face was to him. Yet there was nothing ethereal about it; all was real vitality, real warmth, real incarnation. And it was in her mouth that this culminated . . . her mouth he had seen nothing to equal on the face of the earth. To a young man with the least fire in him that little upward lift in the middle of her red top lip was distracting, infatuating, maddening . . . Perfect, he, as a lover, might have called them off-hand. But no—they were not perfect. And it was the touch of the imperfect upon the would-be perfect that gave the sweetness, because it was that which gave the humanity."
>
> Thomas Hardy, *Tess of the D'Urbervilles*

If you know anything about the urban environment of a mega-city like New York, within the few miles of space between Susan's home and mine were tens of thousands of people. So the geographic proximity of our separate little worlds is noteworthy only because we might just as well have lived 50 or 100 miles away from each other. It just is interesting to me that we lived so close, and yet so far from each other, and our destinies first crossed 100 miles away from both of our homes. Just some trivia . . . not really essential to our love story, but, it's my story isn't it? Stay with me.

Chapter 49

Passion Recalled

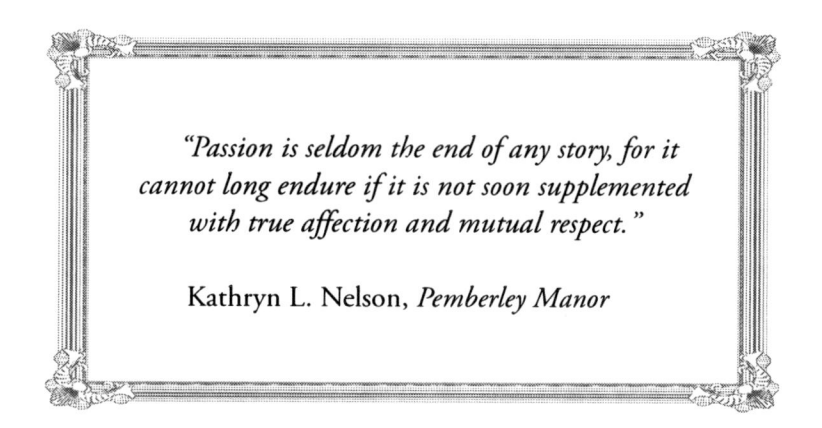

> *"Passion is seldom the end of any story, for it cannot long endure if it is not soon supplemented with true affection and mutual respect."*
>
> Kathryn L. Nelson, *Pemberley Manor*

Yes, we were innocent teenagers when we first met. Susan and I were both virgins, as were most of our contemporaries. However, the emotional damage to Susan that her father's sexual abuse caused was to take a serious toll on our lives from the point of its revelation through every day of our marriage.

When we met, she was 14, I was 16. Of course our generation knew what sex was. Of course young people were titillated by taboo materials, which would pale in comparison to what can be conjured up on the internet today in a matter of seconds.

There was a consistent physical presence of parents in our homes, parents whose marriages remained intact because of the vows of commitment even when perhaps a marital relationship was secretly troubled. And there was an innate respect for womanhood by men and women. Men felt a duty to care for and protect women, and women appreciated it. Women's roles even then were understated in their importance in managing their households and especially guarding and setting their children's moral compasses.

Of course there were exceptions. I'm not trying to describe a heaven on earth. But it was so different from the laxity of moral values that so rapidly began to erode our culture beginning in the 1960s, the years that I was attending college. However, this is not a cultural history lesson. Just a series of snapshots from personally living through a unique period in the history of our so-called modern culture.

Chapter 50

The Delight Of Love

If ever two pairs of lips were meant to enjoy the rapture of kissing, they were Susan's and mine. Her mouth thrilled me to distraction from the very first kiss and throughout our 47 years of married life. She said so many times how she loved my kisses. I was equally thrilled with hers. She would often sigh while we kissed, which caused my heart to melt while other parts hardened. At the time we began dating in the late 1950s, passion rarely went beyond kissing, and my touching her above the waist, through her clothing.

As our relationship progressed and our feelings for each other deepened, our passions while "making out" (that's what it was called then), took us into new territory. This is simply inevitable as a normal young male on the brink of manhood, spends time regularly with a beautiful young female entering womanhood.

I look now at precious old black and white photographs of Susan when she was vibrant, and so young, her life fully ahead of her, so innocent, and so beautiful. I've been remembering the way that being with her caused my heart to beat faster and swell with feelings that I'd never had before. Feelings that pressed in on me causing me to begin to not ever want her to be anywhere but right near me. I yearned to be everything to her; to care for her, to protect her, and to not share her with anyone else, not even her family. Yes, there certainly were sexual desires that were easily unleashed by her physical beauty, and the raging hormones of teenagers, desires that remained in check with great force of will by both of us.

There is an enormous transformational difference in the way men and women grow physically into adulthood. These are generalizations, but I believe that they are true in the majority of cases. After all, I do have eyes in my head, and testosterone in my storage tank.

When a boy grows into an adult male, apart from a deeper voice and more body hair, his physical shape remains essentially the same. Only the proportions change. Yes, he can spend four hours a day in the gym and shoot up with steroids to alter his natural body proportions, but most guys don't do this.

On the contrary, when a girl grows from childhood, through adolescence, and finally to womanhood, major visible changes begin to occur early on. The term "shapeshifter" has become a fairly common science fiction element, overdone in my opinion, but it applies perfectly to females. Females not only shift shapes, they actually seem to grow new body parts! Straight waistlines and legs begin to change into curvaceous accents. Flat chests begin to sprout. Just observe junior high schoolers and you'll see the glaring differences in physical development between teenage boys and girls of the same age. It's as though boys, if they were caterpillars, simply become bigger caterpillars as they grow to adulthood. Yes, there are some very good looking guy caterpillars out there, but, they're still caterpillars. While girls, if they were caterpillars, are the species that transform into butterflies.

I was fortunate enough to know Susan as she was transforming into a beautiful, unique butterfly, right before my eyes. I look at photographs of her as a two-year old, as an eight-year old, as a 14-year old, and thereafter clearly recollect my real life personal observations. Undoubtedly, the lovely butterfly could not be kept from emerging. What's more, as I discovered as our relationship progressed, her inner beauty was every bit as breathtaking as her outer beauty.

An emerging, adorable "butterfly" at two, and the fully shapeshifted, beautiful "butterfly".

I was doomed from the start!!

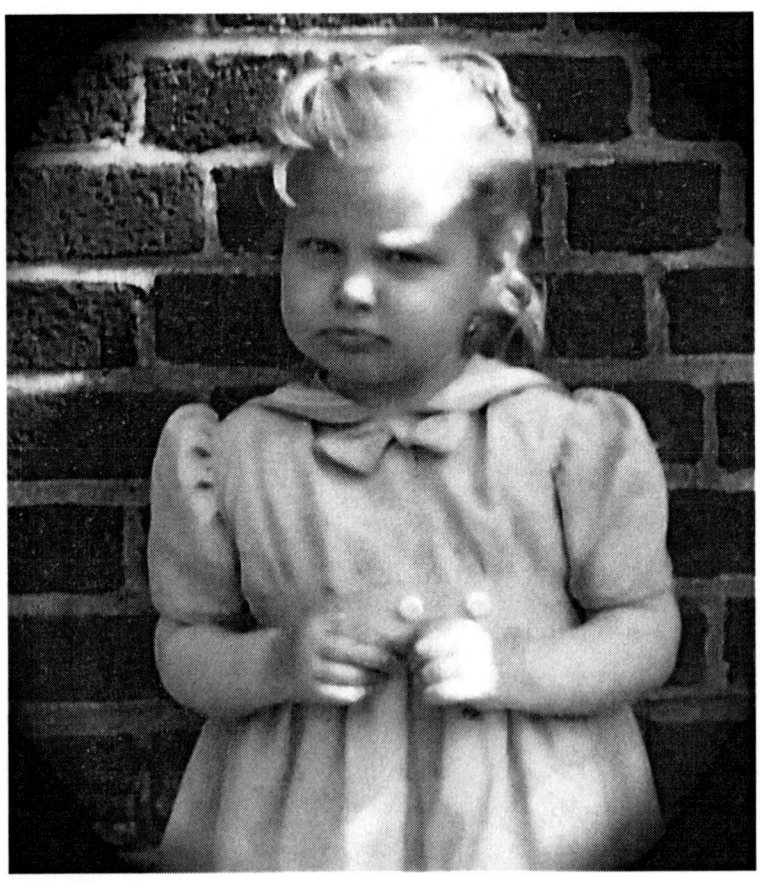

Grumpy Susan at 2

Susan at 17

Susan at 18

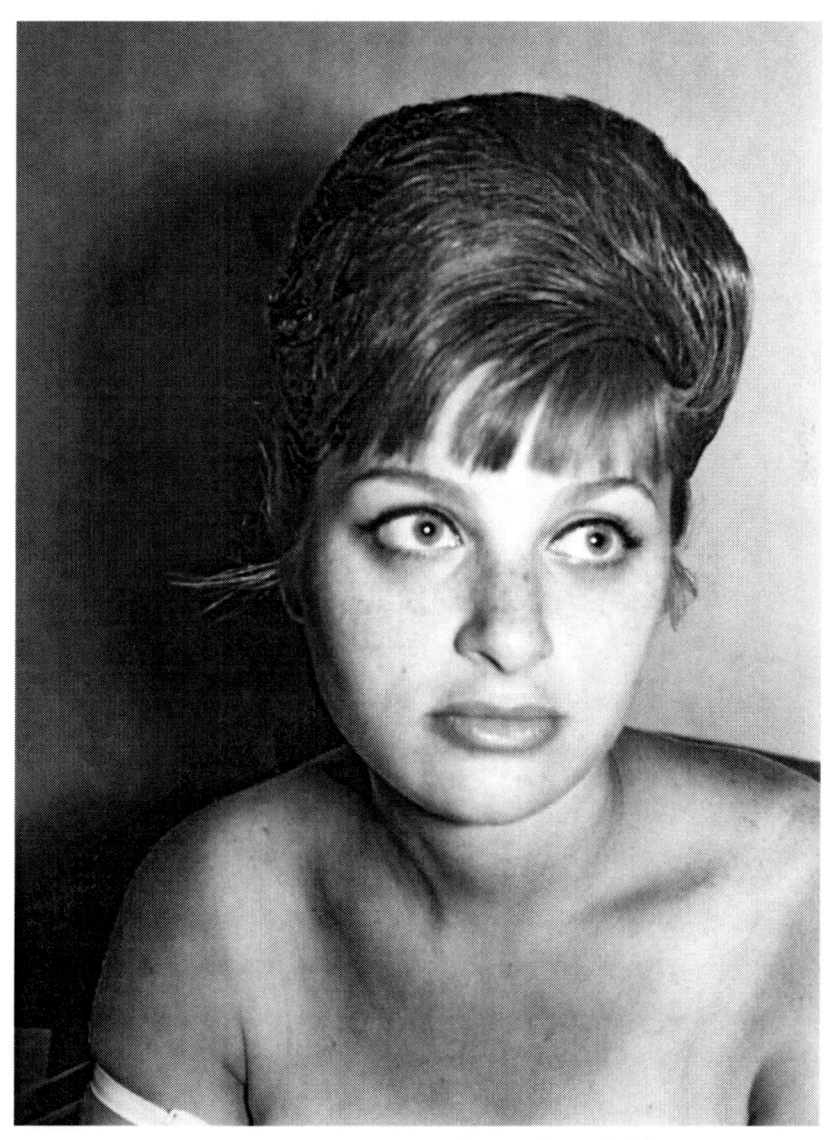

Susan at 25, pregnant with our first child

Chapter 51

Passions Grow

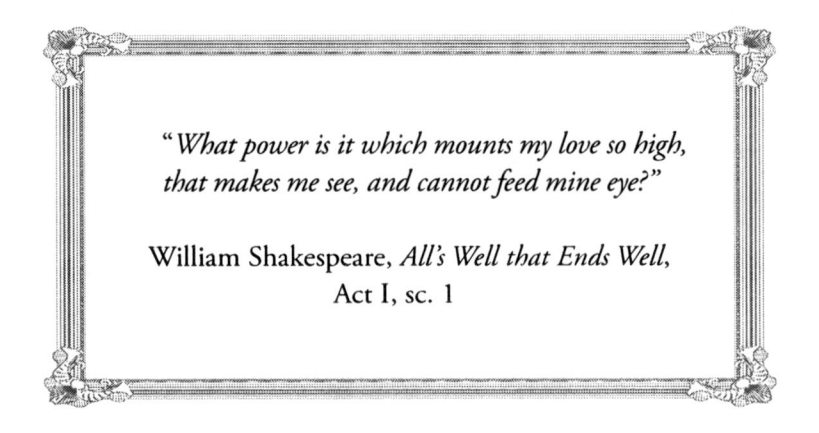

> "*What power is it which mounts my love so high, that makes me see, and cannot feed mine eye?*"
>
> William Shakespeare, *All's Well that Ends Well*, Act I, sc. 1

Though Susan's parents never left us alone at her house, my parents often left us alone at my house. Susan would frequently take the #12A city bus and come to my house on the weekend for the day, stay to have supper with us, and then we would drive her home.

We hoped that my parents would find reason to leave the house, which sometimes occurred for a couple of hours at a time. As soon as the front door closed behind my parents, we were in each other's arms, our yearning mouths locked in delicious, warm kisses, our tongues exploring each other's with moans of delight, our bodies pressed against one another.

Deeper arousal was unavoidable. We would then move to the bed and lie in a tight embrace, continuing our delectable kissing as we became more and more aroused, our breathing accelerating, our kisses more deep and forceful, our bodies pressing ever harder against one another. I would kiss her neck softly and nibble her ear lobes, and she shuddered with pleasure, as did I. I wanted this to never end.

She was in surrender to me, and me to her. She would have allowed me to take whatever I wanted, but I was afraid to pursue intercourse because of cultural and family mores, and out of respect for her vulnerability. With all my heart I wanted to take her, and my body ached for her. But I held back. Up to this point in our relationship there was enough to satisfy my desire. I was with her. We enjoyed being with each other. It didn't seem necessary to take any more of her even though I knew that she would have yielded completely without protest. What we were doing was tantalizing and thrilling enough.

We took advantage of every one of these opportunities when we were alone, which steadily progressed to more intimate touching and the higher levels of pleasure that this brought to both of us. Yet we continued to stop short of intercourse. Until one time, in my house, when we were again alone and at the height of our passions, Susan pleaded with me to take her fully. I was still reluctant. Perhaps it was false gallantry designed to cover my fear of hurting her physically, or a more practical fear of an unintended pregnancy. Both her brothers fathered children out of wedlock.

Here was this beautiful young woman, desperately aroused, asking me to make love to her, her gorgeous blue eyes, her irresistible full mouth, begging me to take her, her arms extended toward me. I could no longer hold myself back. We succumbed to our passions. I felt afraid and guilty. I also felt intoxicatedly wonderful. It was a foretaste of our sexual compatibility. I loved her dearly and did not believe that I had taken advantage of her. She had no regrets afterwards, and this was a great relief for me. It was not just a thrilling physical pleasure. It was a true honor to be the recipient of her passionate surrender, and much more so, this further expression of her love for me.

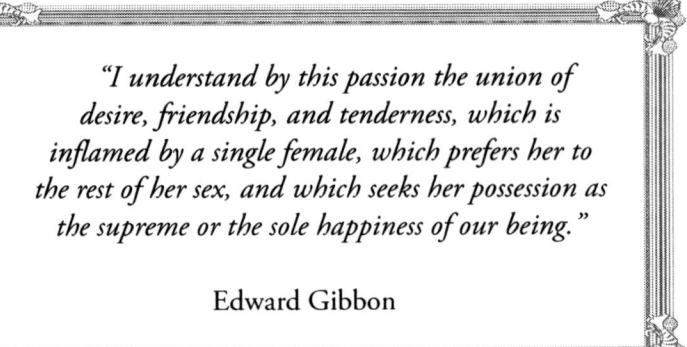

> *"I understand by this passion the union of desire, friendship, and tenderness, which is inflamed by a single female, which prefers her to the rest of her sex, and which seeks her possession as the supreme or the sole happiness of our being."*
>
> Edward Gibbon

Chapter 52

Is My Altered Life Worth Living?

What do I have to live for now that the love of my life, the one and only person that completed me, is gone from my world?

So many times during my days now I find something that I start to tell Susan about, want to talk with her about, want her reaction or opinion, share a joke, discuss current events, talk about our kids and grandkids, on and on. Then I'm cruelly reminded once more that she's gone forever. I miss her so deeply. There is an urge I feel some days during this mournful season of my life to just die. Then I can be with my sweet Susan again.

Then comes a response to this urge each time it sweeps into my heart that reminds me that I still have reasons to remain in the here and now.

My children. My grandchildren. These are very important people in my life. They are reasons for me to be alive.

Susan and I had three wonderful children who we loved dearly, and I still do. Now our children have children of their own, five beautiful grandchildren.

The following are some memories and sentiments that I want my children to know, memorialized in a letter, first to the three of them collectively, then followed by a personal letter to each of them. Perhaps they will share these letters with their children someday.

Maybe there is just a smattering of wisdom here that will bless my children and their children. I hope so.

To my three wonderful children:
Eric, Andrea & Adam

This is not intended as an ominous message so please don't feel the need to brace yourselves. I'm just feeling the rush of time and the desire, therefore, to "chat" with my children. Some of the following may seem to be rambling chunks of thought. But they are the things that as of this moment I feel that God is laying on my heart to share with you. Accept it for what it is, and for what it isn't.

Please don't expect revelatory or brilliant things from me. I don't know that I have anything revelatory or brilliant to offer. What I do offer, though, is a retrospective of a life in its last stage, and I believe that such a retrospective can perhaps be sifted for a few nuggets of value. But that is for you to decide.

I would be thrilled to know that your lives and the lives of my grandchildren will be lives better lived than mine, whether or not anything that I've contributed is worthwhile. You and they can learn just as well by the things that dad or grandpa did that are worthy, as from the things that dad or grandpa did that are unworthy.

As I grow older time seems to move faster. Now it feels like it's rushing by. This is kind of humorous to me because I'm a watch collector who takes great pride in owning precision micro-mechanisms that are designed to regulate time so that little if any of it is lost or gained.

The reality is that regulating time is an illusion. We have no ability to regulate time. Time is out of our control. God Himself lives outside the boundaries of what we know as "time." If anything, time in fact regulates us: When our planet makes its rounds, when we see the sun "come up" and "go down," the changing seasons, our sleep cycles, our wake cycles, the aging process, and so on. One of the silliest things I know is "daylight savings time"... Why not disrupt the entire country twice a year (with an exception or two, e.g., Arizona), for the sake of trying to manipulate one hour of time?

Back to the point: Time for me is rushing by. The end of my life on this planet is closer than ever. That is simply a fact. Sometimes it bothers me, most of the time now it does not. With whatever time on Earth that I have left, I have boiled my personal hopes down to three things:

1) *To be closer to God on a daily basis.*

2) *To know His peace in all circumstances.*

3) *To have my needs met.*

No, this isn't a suicide note and as of the moment I don't have any life-threatening illness that I'm aware of. Yet speaking factually, I am indeed nearing the end of my life. I'm 70 years old as I write this.

You might say that 70 is not very old these days, especially based on the fact that my father lived in relatively good health until almost 94, and my mother until 92. Yet, recent statistics on mortality state that on average, a white male, age 65, in the U.S. can expect to live 82.2 years. If these statistics are borne out in my life, then 85% of my life has already been lived. This is a sobering thought, though I realize that I could actually live to be 100, or die before I finish writing this letter.

And the rest of my life no matter how long or short may be substantially affected by the quality of my life, the earthly limitations of mental and/or physical functionality. So if I feel that I'd like to try to communicate lucidly with you, better sooner than later, for who knows what I'll be capable of tomorrow? Perhaps that's why I'm feeling God's prompt at this time.

What is it that I wish to say to you as I near the end of life? Maybe I shouldn't even bother grappling with this question. Why say anything at all? Maybe, no matter what I come up with, it really won't make any difference in the scheme of things. Am I wanting to make a difference? Do I dare to imagine that I can make a difference? After all, doesn't history continually repeat itself? No matter how clear the lessons of history, we, as humankind, make the same mistakes over and over again. Pretty sad, huh? And we're supposed to be the most superior creation of God on this Earth, "Man".

It used to be—"back in the day" as the expression goes—when families lived very near to one another for most if not all of their lives, intimate discussions occurred regularly, typically around the kitchen table, at grandma and grandpa's house, or aunt and uncle so-and-so's house, during frequent visits, and at vacation places where the family would gather for memory-making. These were life-shaping experiences, although at the time the younger folks didn't know that what we were experiencing was to be life-shaping.

But our modern world doesn't permit us to do this nearly as much. Right now is typical of our family's dispersion…our culture's dispersion. With Adam currently looking for another job, and living temporarily a couple of hours away in the interim, who knows where he and his family will end up. I'm a cross-country trip away from Andrea and family, as well as from Eric and Mariah. This is considerably distant and costly, especially now that my income has been substantially reduced.

Not only is it impractical and expensive to try to all be together in the same place on a regular basis, or even once every year or two, it is becoming less and less physically reasonable for me to make such trips.

So what are the alternatives? Video phone calls are wonderful but pale in comparison to our being together in the flesh. Though also a weak substitute for being with you all face-to-face, I feel led to try to put some thoughts in writing. They may have little or no positive impact on you and your families but I feel the desire to do this. Perhaps I have a distorted view of self-importance. Or maybe I'm just yielding to my nature because I find it cathartic to express my feelings in writing. Or maybe I just care about you so much that I'm desperately wanting you to gain something from my stumblings and bumblings.

Maybe, just maybe, there will be enough sense and sensibility found in the few windows of thought that I offer that you won't fall prey to the same mistakes that I've made, and so, true evolution will occur, an evolution to a better quality of life for you, your children and their children.

Often I've wondered how much of my heart and mind to share with my children. After all, I come out of the "Silent Generation," which means, those who just do what needs to be done without talking much about it. Yep, it's the Nike slogan: "Just Do It." And though I don't know how my parent's generation is characterized—everything needs a label it seems—they certainly never spoke to their children about their hopes, dreams and fears. Of course, when children are very young this is probably a wise course to follow. After all, what frame of reference does a small child have for adult issues, which can also be frightening to young children? But when children grow into adulthood, say by age 15, or 16 and older, is it appropriate for parents to begin to share such things with them? I believe that the answer to this question is, yes.

Because, if kids are left to learn only from inference, and from observed subtleties (and here I'm referring to learning from their parents) that can be a hit or miss proposition. What is more important for a person to learn: the ABCs, algebra, grammar, history, or, real life lessons? ... how to live a life, or not to live a life ... learned from the people closest to them; from those persons with the most influence to bring to bear: their parents.

Now, these lessons may be good ones or bad ones, or realistically, a probable mixture of both. Learning takes place whether or not the lesson is one with a happy outcome or a sad outcome. I will suggest to you that the most important work of parenting is to train up the next generation to 'do it better.' Of course the 'it' is an important factor. So let's just assume here that the 'it' is a good thing. Many might say that love is the most important thing that parents can provide to their children. Of course, this is a monumentally important factor. Yet I wonder: What can be more loving than enabling your children to fulfill their lives with greater success than you have managed, along with the parental nurture that they also need? What can be more beneficial to humankind than to have adult children who are able to contribute more positively to our world than their parents did, and to then 'pay it forward' to succeeding generations?

I'm rather convinced that it is better to open my heart to you more, rather than less, especially now that you are all adults, I am a card-carrying senior citizen, and because two of you are raising your own young children. This is not to diminish or exclude Eric and Mariah, because I want them to know my heart as much as I want Andrea and Jeff, and Adam and Shantel to know my heart. It is simply that having young children now to guide through life adds a special burden for parents. Though raising children is a unique and important role, we still influence some, or perhaps many other people by the way we live our lives. Brothers, sisters, nieces, nephews, friends, neighbors, coworkers, and so on. Even our parents. If you've ever participated in psychological group counseling, as I have, it would not be unusual to hear peoples' stories peppered with how this or that person, not necessarily a parent, impacted their lives forever, for better or for worse.

We all criticize our parents for trivial as well as important things, don't we? Perhaps with good reasons. I've done it and still find myself blaming my mom and dad for this or that from time to time. God, it's an awful and sad fact of life! Do parents ever get paroled or pardoned from the sentences that their offspring pronounce against them? Do children ever feel that it's time to let go of painful memories attributed to their parents? How often do parents truly deserve a life sentence for some shortcoming that they couldn't have accomplished better if they had it to do over a thousand times because they just didn't have the equipment to make it happen differently? Why are we so much more willing to forgive virtual strangers for offenses they bring upon us than to forgive our own parents, or our own children?

I don't have any definitive answers to these questions, but I believe that part of the reason may be that we expect from our earthly parents the things that only our heavenly Father can provide. Earthly parents are doomed to the failure of imperfection because the first earthly parents were so doomed. Just look at the offspring of Adam and Eve and the terrible outcomes suffered by that family. The gross imperfections of family relationships have been historically perpetuated, as the Scriptures and other historical texts record ad infinitum.

In the spirit of opening my heart to my children, here's a brief sketch of my present circumstances.

As Ecclesiastes states, there is a season for all things. At this moment in time my heart is very heavy for a number of reasons. Your mom, the love of my life, died five months ago, and I am still in an emotional fog. Accordingly my future is clouded by mostly unknown or hard to face possibilities. My financial future is less secure than it was because of the current economic downturn and the impact its had on our retirement savings and our home equity, which is completely gone, and now, the loss of mom's Social Security income benefit. We've always been responsible with our money and now I have a compelling need to reduce expenditures quite a lot in order to help my resources to last longer. This means: I will travel less. I will buy less for myself and my loved ones. I've dropped insurance policies that are less than essential. We sold our second car. I'm working on liquidating my watch and firearms collections.

I've been looking for employment and recently decided that if possible I would consider going back to work full-time even if it means relocating. Part-time professional jobs are not out there for me and so I am also applying for unskilled part-time work such as at local retail stores. This is very humbling for me but I'm willing to do what may be necessary to help my circumstances. From my experience job-searching the past year or two the probability of my being hired in any paying job is about zero.

This isn't what mom and I expected our retirement to be like, but this is reality. There are days for me that are dominated by anger, fear, frustration and deep sadness. Though I have drawn closer to the Lord, and feel less and less attached to material things, this is not what I would call a happy time. I miss my sweet Susan so much that it brings on physical pain most days. Right now I'm very vulnerable.

There are great moments or events in everyone's life. One should hope that in their life there is a truly Greatest moment.

As memory best serves me there certainly have been great moments and events in my life. Many I've probably forgotten by now, because though exciting at the time, not all of them were worthy of lifelong vividness. What may seem great at the time, for example, to an eight year old, becomes only at best a warm recollection years later. To illustrate.

There was my very special black and red snow sled with the steerable third runner in front, so unlike all my friends' sleds. And it was faster than all the other sleds too. My friends were in awe. Then there was the cast metal water pistol that projected farther and held more water than any of the plastic garden variety water pistols that other kids had. I never, ever saw another one like it. Getting a puppy, our Cocker Spaniel, Ginger, was a truly great moment. My Bar Mitzvah, reaching adulthood in the Jewish faith, and all the special training and hard work that was required. Working at various fun, but not so important jobs while in high school and college. Excelling in schoolyard sports. Being captain of my high school rifle team. Summer camp as a counselor, the only time in my life that this city boy got to go to sleep-away camp. What a great summer! A summer as a busboy at a resort hotel in the Catskill Mountains, New York. Girlfriends. First love. Attending and graduating college. Courting your mother. Being married. Having children. Starting and succeeding at a career. If I took enough time there would be many, many more intersecting events that would continue to reflect a lifeline of great and even greater moments and events.

But the greatest thing, the truly Greatest moment and Greatest event in my life was when I met Jesus Christ, Jesus the Messiah, and accepted Him as my Savior. Nothing comes close to comparing with this. Nothing will ever come close. Nothing could come close. Nothing should come close. This was a truly supernatural experience that must be noted as the zenith of my life, no matter how long I may live in this earthly body. For how can one even attempt to compare a personal rendezvous with the Creator of the universe, the Author of all life, the King of all kings, with anything else?

There is however something that is important to position alongside this amazing event, in the sense that it has a comparable context. And this has become more evident to me as the years have gone by. That is, my wife and my children also accepting Jesus as their Lord and Savior. I take no credit as the choreographer of such joyous, and eternally momentous events, yet I know that I was a conduit that permitted the Lord to do His work in the lives of my family. Search the Scriptures and you will not have much difficulty finding many terribly imperfect people, like me, used by God to facilitate wonderful works. If I'd somehow stood in the way, God would have found another way to accomplish His purpose. From the moment that Jesus was accepted as Savior by my wife and my children, God the Father became the perfect father that they never had. And I, knowing how imperfect I am as a father and husband, am so utterly grateful for God's intervention in our lives. This caused me to think about 'free will'.

There is a great difference between free will and free choice. You see, we all are given 'free will' by our Creator God, to do anything that is within our realm of mortal power to accomplish, whether good or evil. But we do not have free choice. Let me explain.

When faced with a do-I-go-left? or, do-I go-right? decision, we have the freedom of will to do either, whether or not the consequences of each choice are clear at the time of our decision. That is what I believe to be 'free will'. Do I lie or do I tell the truth? Do I steal or restrain my temptation? Do I cheat on the exam or study harder? Do I do this or do I do that? To the extent that the alternatives are real enough that you can make any of them happen, then you are dealing with free will.

But 'free choice' is different, and far more restrictive. We simply do not have the free choice to do anything that we want to do. If I don't have the intellect to successfully study and absorb science, I cannot choose to become a physician, or chemist, or biologist, no matter how much I might want to. If as an adult my height is five feet four inches, I likely cannot choose to be a professional basketball player. If I'm born Hispanic I cannot choose to be Caucasian. If I'm born female, notwithstanding the modern radical applications of medical science, I cannot choose to be male, or vice versa.

I am your earthly father and you had no choice in the matter. Your free will permits you to relate with me in any way you'd like, but you have no choice about who the father is with whom you will relate. Our relationship will always be imperfect, because we are imperfect. We are simply incapable of anything else but imperfect behaviors.

Even in the only relationship you will ever have in which at least one of you is truly perfect—your relationship with God—think about how often that relationship is in turmoil. Why? Because as long as one party to a relationship is less than perfect, there will be trouble in that relationship. When both parties are imperfect, it is truly miraculous that positive outcomes can occur in any human relationship more than on the rarest occasions!

And so it is. You have an imperfect earthly father (me), as all of us have or have had, but you also have a perfect Father. How blessed you are! Someday when we are all in Heaven together we will understand all things, including how unimportant so many earthly things were, especially those things that created barriers between us during our precious short lives on Earth together. Because God tells us that there will be no pain in Heaven, I believe that we won't suffer from the knowledge of our missteps that we will then obtain. What a great God we have! But it sure causes pain and suffering on this side of Heaven, doesn't it?

It is a mystery to me: Why is life so full of trials and pain? Why didn't God create Man with 'perfect will' in addition to free will? Why does the story of history have to be so full of repeated tragedy? Why couldn't Heaven be Heaven from the beginning of awareness throughout eternity? Only God knows the answers to these questions, and someday I believe that we will clearly see the perfection of God's plans.

These days, inside the rush of time, I've been finding myself overcome with regret and sadness. I've always found a way to succeed in just about everything I've done. But, parenting, ah, that stands in a realm of its own, and I know that I have not earned high marks as a parent. I can't do it over, but you can do it better. I ask you, my dear children: How often have you questioned your abilities to be good parents, not great parents, but just good parents? How many times have you regretted the way you've responded to your children? How often have you responded to your child in anger? Have you always meted out punishment with fairness and objectivity? Have you mastered the concept of firm but fair? Have you ever deprived your children of the degree of affection and understanding that their perfect Father stands ready to give them every moment of every day, and that they desperately need from you? Are you always teaching your children the right lessons by commission or omission? Either by your words or actions are you ashamed of things you've done to, or in view of, your children? Is it rare or common that you feel inadequate as a parent? Does parenthood feel stifling at times? Frightening at times? Overwhelming at times? Does parenthood interfere with your relationship with your spouse and the quality of that relationship including your intimacy? Have you realized yet that parenting never ends as long as you and your children are alive?

OK, so being a parent is a tremendously daunting job, and probably few people get anywhere close to a perfect score. But even the ones who get it mostly right don't necessarily have children who turn out to be great contributors to humankind. That's another mystery that I won't even begin to delve into because, here again, I don't have the answers. Don't worry, I'm not building toward pointing a finger at any of you. In fact I am extremely proud of the three of you and the quality people that you have developed into, likely in spite of me, rather than because of me.

You are very capable, intelligent and responsible people, and you are all quite independent of parental management now and have been for some time, and that is the way it should be. I try not to insert myself into your business unless invited to, although sometimes I am so terribly tempted to jump in to try to save you from yourselves. But that's not really my role any longer.

You have your marriages to work on, children to raise, other family members to relate with, bodies, minds and spirits to keep healthy, jobs to perform, friendships to grow, hopes and dreams to ponder, and hopefully a vibrant relationship with God that you are weaving into the complicated tapestries of your lives. The last thing that I'd ever want to do is to make these things even more difficult for you to accomplish.

The following are brief letters to each of you, containing a few tidbits of memories, and expressions of how proud and happy I am to have lived to see the fine people that you have each developed into. I know that mom would agree completely. Whether you would agree or not you were blessed to have an extraordinary mother who often compensated for a less than extraordinary father.

I so dearly hope and pray that I can be a welcome part of each of your lives, or at the very least, a part of your lives that you will tolerate with Godly patience. Whether or not it has always seemed so to you, I have always wanted only the best for each of you, and I still do. I regularly pray for your well-being and the well-being of your families.

I now pray: May your marriages be anointed and protected by God. May your children be centered in God's hands and grow to know Him as Lord of their lives. May you find God's peace no matter what your circumstances may be until this world passes on to the world without end, and within which you all have the ultimate assurance of perfect lives, eternal peace, and never ending joy, even though I'll be there too!

The following is one of the most important scripture verses in my life. It helps to guide me and to strengthen my faith when my faith walk gets off course, which is fairly often. Mom embroidered this and had it framed for me. It hung in my office in a very prominent place for many years.

I'm sure that you are familiar with this verse and hope that it will be as meaningful to you as it has been to me.

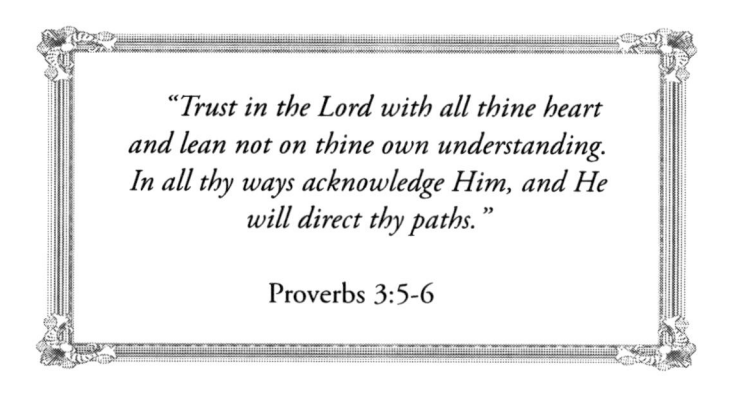

> "Trust in the Lord with all thine heart and lean not on thine own understanding. In all thy ways acknowledge Him, and He will direct thy paths."
>
> Proverbs 3:5-6

With much love,
Your earthly father

Dear Eric,

You are our firstborn child and that will always be a unique position in your life. Unfortunately, when parents leave the hospital with a newborn child, they don't receive a child-rearing manual, nor are they required to take classes to learn how to be a good parent. Many mistakes are made, especially with a first-born child, because you become the first test case in the family unit.

You showed unusual intelligence from a very early age, performing many things ahead of the curve such as walking, talking, memorizing, and reading. Your love of reading has followed you into adulthood. You were an easy child to raise because you were mild-mannered and obedient. If we asked you to play in your room, that's what you did. We often took you with us to visit friends and you were not fussy and could easily sleep wherever we happened to be when your bedtime arrived.

You were not easily distracted, possessing an unusually strong ability to focus your attention for long periods of time on things that interested you.

Remember, when you were about six or seven I think, I took you shopping to the Venture store near where we lived in St. Louis, and I left you in the toy section while I shopped around the store? I completely forgot about you and drove home without you. Mom was enraged when we realized that I'd left you in the store, so I rushed back, about a 10 minute drive, and there you were, still examining toys in the toy section. You didn't even know that I'd left without you.

No, you weren't an angel on earth. You got into fights with other kids, and racked up your share of mischief. But all-in-all, you were no real trouble, and this fact encouraged us to have more children.

Because you were an obedient child we might have recognized early on that you would make an excellent soldier, which you indeed were for 24 years. You inherited some of grandpa Dick's, and I suppose some of my, genes for drawing and for precision. You use these gifts to have fun with pencil and paper and to build and decorate scale models. And your proclivity for precision is aptly applied in your new civilian career as a technical writer.

You have always had a tendency to keep your own counsel: Working out your life-issues as best you can without depending on others to solve things for you. Sometimes this made us wonder if you valued knowing our opinions. I believe that you simply prefer to solve your own problems. There are probably many things that you have tucked away in secret places in your head that we never knew, and probably that is just as well.

You did very well in school. Learning came very easily to you and we expected that you would eventually go on to get a college degree. You have a knack for writing and we weren't surprised that you chose to attend the University of Missouri in Columbia, MO, in hopes of being accepted into their renowned journalism program. It was during your freshman year that I accepted a promotion and we were going to be relocating to Portland, Oregon. In retrospect I believe that this event threw you a major curve ball. You dropped out of college and came to live with us in Portland, spending a lot of time in your room reading, and working at jobs that were menial for you.

After almost a year of seeing you in limbo I suggested to you that you consider joining the military as a way to use your energy to serve your country and to perhaps discover what you want to do with your life. Being the obedient child that you were, soon after our conversation, you joined the U.S.A.F., beginning a career that much to our surprise lasted 24 years, taking you all over the world, including a frightening (for us) tour of duty at the very early stages of the first Gulf War.

Mom and I were so thankful that you returned from the war with no physical injuries. However, it saddens me that in a recent conversation when I asked you if you suffered any Post Traumatic Stress following your military service, you indicated that you did, and are being medically treated for your symptoms.

Your steady rise through the ranks to ultimately retire as a Master Sergeant made us very proud of your accomplishments. Your sense of responsibility and independence are traits that mom and I greatly admired. Your sense of humor is a joy.

Of course we know how much you tortured your brother, Adam, six years younger than you. But, hey, what are younger brothers for anyway? As far as we know, Adam suffered no lasting scars, physical or emotional.

I am very proud of who you are, I always have been, and mom would be in complete agreement. What a joy you were as a bright, inquisitive, and quick-to-learn child. How well you served your country in wartime and peacetime, how you've worked through difficult challenges in your life, your rededication to getting your bachelor's degree, and how well you've transitioned to civilian life. And I am blessed that you now call me regularly to check up on me.

With much love,
Dad

Dear Andrea,

Our second child, our only daughter. I remember when you were two or three years old that you already had a very determined personality. My mother said to me at this early time in your life that you were going to be a handful. This was when she and grandpa Dick stayed at our apartment in Massachusetts to babysit you and Eric while mom and I went for a few days of vacation which we'd not done in a long time. Grandma Fay was right on the money.

As the Scripture says, we are all uniquely and wonderfully made! I was a strong-willed person when I reached adulthood, yet when I was a child, I was submissive and respectful to my parents. When I was told 'no', it was 'no'. Not so with you, dear daughter. You often did not accept 'no', and did so with much emotional energy. This trait only strengthened as you got older. Remember the times that mom and I hired babysitters so that we could sneak out to dinner once in a while? Remember telephoning us at the restaurant to tell us that the sitter was being horrible to you? That's when we stopped telling you where we were going out to eat.

You were, and still are, a very bright, inquisitive person, logical, and well-organized, and did well in school until your freshman year of high school when we moved from St. Louis, Missouri, to Portland, Oregon, because of my job promotion. You cried when we showed you Wilson High School, the school you would be attending.

You were overwhelmed by its size compared with the high school you would have attended in St. Louis, and you had a difficult time adjusting to our move. Probably as an act of rebellion, you did not do well academically, started to hang out with kids on the margins, and informed us that after graduating high school you were going to marry some yutz that was your then current boyfriend.

This was all happening after we took into our home, at your urging, Rene Johanson, a 15 year old girl whom you'd met in school, who was pregnant. You asked us to give her a place to live until she could find a more permanent arrangement. Rene was adopted by alcoholic parents who told her that they regretted adopting her, insisted she have an abortion or get out of their home, and her brother was a drug dealer. She'd spent a lot of time on the streets with similarly troubled kids who we got to know very well because our home became a sanctuary for them.

You shared your room with Rene, who had her baby boy, Shane, while she lived with us as our foster daughter. Rene remained with us off and on for five or six years with Shane. You told mom and me that Rene's life was a dramatic example to you of what you would never want to happen in your life. This was quite an object lesson in life, realtime!

Well, things don't often go as planned, and thank God for that. Your boyfriend dumped you and after you cried bitter tears about it, the very same night of the breakup you asked me if I would take you and Rene to see a movie. Imagine that . . . a 15 year old girl wanting to go on a date, in public, with her daddy! Crazy talk! I was thrilled, and we had a great time.

Soon after all this you rededicated your life to Christ and decided that you wanted to go to college. After only a couple of years in Portland, I also rededicated my life to Christ, and I left my lucrative job to go to work for one of the finest Christian liberal arts colleges in the country, Westmont College, in Santa Barbara, California. You weren't ready academically for the rigorous program at Westmont, so you enrolled at Santa Barbara City College to ease your way into the world of higher education. You did well and transferred to Westmont the following year, ultimately graduating with a B.A. in Sociology, then going on to get a Master's Degree from Brandeis University. Who woulda thunk!

Your strong-willed persona ultimately brought wonderful dividends for you, and blessings to your parents: A 'sister', Rene, your first 'nephew', Shane, invaluable first-hand observation of the underbelly of life based on the choices people make, a new respect and desire for education, a determination to get your bachelor's degree from Westmont College, and to our surprise, a desire for a post-grad degree.

While pursuing your graduate program at Brandeis University, you met Jeffrey Yepez, your future husband, and now you are a devoted wife, and mother to Gabriel and Joshua, two beautiful, healthy, and bright boys. When you met Jeff and your relationship became serious, you accepted the fact that he had four daughters from his previous marriage who would be a regular part of your lives for many years to come, the youngest being five at the time you were married.

You never flinched from this enormous responsibility, giving love, and nurture to these girls. The oldest, Kristina, chose to come to live with you and Jeff when she turned 18 and is now a senior in college, still living with your family.

I am so proud of who you are and know that mom would agree wholeheartedly: How you have grown through intelligent analysis of life's realities, asking lots of questions . . . oh, and I do mean lots of questions . . . developing a close, special, girl-to-girl relationship with your mom, usually making the right choices though preferring a lot of space to work them through, and the admirable path that you have chosen for your life, foregoing a working career that you trained for, to instead devoting yourself to your husband and children.

With much love,
Dad

Dear Adam,

Our third, and last child, our younger son. Of the three of you, you are the closest to being a broad composite of all the members of our immediate family.

Eric and Andrea look more like me than they look like mom. You have facial features that swing more to resembling mom. Eric is quiet and sensitive, not in a cowering way, but he just has a laid-back demeanor. Andrea is the direct opposite of Eric; she has a very strong-willed persona, often challenging this or that, able and willing to be cleverly difficult, even at a very early age.

You are a little of all of your siblings' traits, and some of mom and me as well. You were outwardly more aggressive than your brother, but not stubborn. You were able to accept 'no' as 'no', and just shake it off, in this way much like your brother. You gravitated to sports, playing youth soccer, then high school soccer, and also played little league baseball, while at the same time wanting to learn to play the guitar. We counseled you to hold off on the guitar until something dropped off your plate.

Thus, you were a natural born multi-tasker, more like your sister, and your mother. Eric preferred to dig in deep on one thing at a time, was more cerebral than you, and never had much interest in playing organized sports.

You were a very sociable kid ... still are! Even while playing youth soccer and baseball, you seemed to enjoy just being with other kids as much as you were interested in playing the game to win, or becoming an exceptional athlete. If your team lost, and I remember a soccer season when your team didn't win a single game, it didn't seem to matter all that much to you, you were just having fun. Mom and I loved that about you and we enjoyed watching you have fun playing ball, often waving to us from your position on the playing field.

You grew to be big-boned and physically strong by the time you were in high school. Yet you had a compassionate heart. I remember a time during a soccer game when an opposing team player was injured running into you. It was like he hit a stone wall. You were proud of your ability to play such strong defense, but you were also concerned about the injured player, who had no serious injuries.

You were very outgoing, made friends easily, and had a large circle of friends. You seemed to have a discerning spirit about who to choose as a friend, even at a young age. You did a lot of volunteer work with a large church in Santa Barbara where you met many of the people who would become lifelong friends. You are still in contact with many of those guys and gals, all of whom, to the best of my knowledge, are doing well in their lives.

Working hard at your studies and your recreational pursuits was your trademark. You enjoyed giving all things your all. When you finally found the desire to play the guitar too compelling to put off any longer, you taught yourself to play by just plunking away until you could make music. Little did we expect that you would become accomplished enough as a musician to write, produce, and record your own compositions, and to also become a worship arts pastor in your career journey in church leadership.

Much like your sister, you first attended Santa Barbara City College for a year or so, and then transferred to Westmont College where you earned a Bachelor's degree in Religious Studies. After Westmont you went on to pursue and attain a Master of Theology degree from Talbot Seminary as part of your preparation to equip yourself for your calling as a pastor.

While at Talbot you attended a church where you met Shantel Reynolds, who would become your future wife and the devoted mother of your three beautiful, bright, and healthy children, Sadie, Dillon, and Logan.

You have become a committed man of God, seeking to serve His church, which is His people here on Earth. With broad experience in church service both as a volunteer and as a paid staff member, you have a very meaty resumé to offer in God's service.

I am very proud of the man who you have become, and without question, mom would say amen to this. You continue to exhibit the resilience, optimism, and penchant for hard work that you exhibited as a young child, and then consistently maintained as you grew to adolescence, and then adulthood, even in the face of prolonged trials. Your self-taught musical gift still amazes me when I listen to you play the guitar, especially when you play your own musical compositions.

I am especially grateful to you for your willingness to come alongside me when mom was dying in the hospital, to be with me as she drew her last breath on Earth, and to continue to be at my side after mom died to help me deal with overwhelming issues at a time when I could barely think straight. There are no words adequate enough to express my deep appreciation to you for your monumental act of courage, maturity, and love, when I needed it so desperately, and while you too were suffering the onset of grief.

With much love
Dad

Chapter 53

Letters To Grandchildren

This book is dedicated first to my dear wife Susan, then to my three wonderful children, and my five beautiful grandchildren: Jeffrey Gabriel ("Gaby", 7 1/2), Joshua Andrew ("Josh", 5 1/2), Sadie Elise (6), Dillon Ellis (3 1/2), and Logan Reed (1 1/2).

I wrote this book because I want Susan's memory to live on in the hearts and minds of others, especially my children and grandchildren.

I have included letters in this book written to my children. I now want to write something to each of my grandchildren, who are so special to me, things that you will understand more fully when you are older.

Dear Grandchildren,

I love each one of you very much. You are the children of my children, and you have added extraordinary blessings to my life. We are blood relatives, therefore, some of our genetic qualities are shared. Family members are connected by blood and by other chemistry that God places within us. This means, that in a very real way, when a blood relative dies, although it is very sad, part of that person still lives on inside of you. Therefore, part of grandma Susan lives in each of you, and this should help you to be even better people as you find your way in our world, because she was a wonderful person.

One of the saddest things I've had to deal with is that your wonderful grandma Susan died when you were all so young. So, some of you will not remember her at all. I so wish that this was not true, because she was such a dear, loving, person, who was so very happy when she was with her grandchildren. Just look at her face in this photo.

Susan with grandchildren (left to right) Dillon, Logan and Sadie

I hope that someday when you are old enough, you will each read this book that I wrote about my life with grandma Susan, and that the book will be a link between you and her, and someday between your children and their great grandmother, and great grandfather, Susan and Bob.

There are a few things that I'd like to say to each of you in an open letter so that you may each read all the letters. I know that grandma Susan would fully agree with what I have written to you.

The Bible says that we are each uniquely and wonderfully made. Each of you is different, just like every snowflake is different. This is God's way of enriching the Earth that He created with billions of people, all with differences from one another. Not even identical twins are truly identical in every way. This shows God's power, His creativity, and His joy, in making each person different. Each of you is different from your brothers, sister, cousins, and from every other person in the world.

Dear Gabriel,

You are our first grandchild, now almost eight years old. Being our first grandchild will always make you unique among my other four grandchildren. You are inquisitive, intelligent, and comfortable being with other children, even girls, which is unusual for someone your age, but certainly not a negative attribute. I love the times we spent together at your house in Bedford, sitting on the floor building Lego projects in the upstairs play area. Mostly, I watched you engrossed in your activity, and I handed you the pieces you wanted. You are creative, and this will be a valuable trait as you grow into manhood. It will allow you to find alternatives to challenges that others might not see. You love school, and this too is very gratifying to me, and I know your parents feel the same way too. Education is so important to living a worthwhile life. Your creativity and intelligence, if well-applied, will make a wonderful difference in our world.

You are impatient and sometimes explosive in how you express yourself. Guess who you resemble most when these traits pop up? Your wonderful mom! (And your grandpa Bob.) See what I mean about shared genetic traits? I've sensed that you've mellowed a bit as you've gotten older ... that's a good thing. When I talk with your parents on the phone, I often hear you and Josh yelling in the background. It makes me laugh. It's natural for brothers to compete with one another; My brother and I did the same thing when we were kids and shared a room and toys.

Whether you know it or not, your little brother looks up to you and he wants to do the things that you do. I hope that you and Josh will grow to be close friends. The two of you are in a very unique relationship. Though you have four wonderful half-sisters, you and Josh are the only two offspring of your mom and dad. Take good care of each other. Take care of your little brother. Practice self-control. It will make you a better person and more effective in applying your mind to anything you choose to tackle.

I look forward with great excitement to see the wonderful things that I know you will do with your life as you grow older.

Love,
Grandpa

Dear Sadie,

You are our second grandchild, now six years old, our only granddaughter. This makes you unique among our four male grandchildren. Grandma Susan and I were thrilled to have a granddaughter in the family, particularly one as special as you are. Its remarkable how different girls are from boys. You are all girl! You developed verbal communication skills at a high level very early in your life, and even today, your vocabulary and the maturity of your thought processes, and your sense of humor, amaze and amuse me. The way you change your outfits often several times a day is so 'girlie', and it is so much fun to see what you're going to come out wearing next.

It was an unexpectedly exciting event when you decided to cut your own hair a while back. You wanted to look more like your mommy, and I'm sure that she was very flattered . . . after she got over the shock. The pictures I have of you when mommy took you to her hairdresser to fix up your haircut are very precious photos that I will always enjoy looking at with a big smile on my face. You're doing well in school and enjoying the beginnings of your formal education. This is very gratifying to me, and it was a joy too for grandma Susan. By the way, you are also very beautiful, and I'm sure that you will break many boys' hearts as you grow older.

You like to be in charge. This is not unusual because you are the oldest child. But I think it is also a part of your natural personality. It will be very interesting to see what you decide to do with your life when you are older. I always wished that I could have had an older sister. Older sisters are kind of like second moms. God designed women with a stronger desire than men, to care for other people, especially their own children. Don't be surprised if someday, when the three of you are older, that your younger brothers will look up to you in a very special way as their big sister who they can come to for advice and the special love that only a big sister can give to them. Be kind to them, watch over them, and help them to learn by sharing the things you learn in school.

*Love,
Grandpa Bob*

Dear Josh,

You are our third grandchild, almost six years old, just a few months younger than your cousin Sadie. As I wrote in my letter to Gaby, God made every person different. So, even though you have the same mom and dad as Gaby, you are very different than he is. And that is a wonderful thing. When grandma Susan and I visited you we were amazed at how easily you climbed on everything. You're just a natural climber and you do it with no fear ... but sometimes I'm sure your parents are worried that you might get hurt. During one of our visits to your house in Bedford, I remember you falling off the chair at one of the computers. You were probably about two years old at the time. You landed on your head and screamed and cried. We took you to the hospital to get you checked out. Fortunately, you had no serious injury. Who knows, maybe someday you'll climb Mt. Everest, the tallest mountain on Earth. That would really be something, huh? I'm going to take a guess and say that I think you will be a good athlete. You may like gymnastics. Did you know that your mom took gymnastic lessons when she was a young girl?

You recently started school and mom tells me that you like it. You are a smart boy, like your brother, and I'm sure that you will do very well in school. I'm very impressed with the things that you build with Legos. I have a photo of you on my refrigerator, holding the motorcycle that you made. I'm very proud of your accomplishment! I especially enjoy talking with you on the phone. Gaby doesn't seem to like talking on the phone very much, but you don't seem to mind. It makes me feel closer to you when we talk and that is a very wonderful feeling for a grandpa.

I hope that I'll be seeing you, Gaby, and mom and dad soon, in your new home on Maui. You can show me around and we can go to the beach together. I can hardly wait.

Love,
Grandpa

Dear Dillon,

You are our fourth grandchild, now almost three and a half years old. Mommy and daddy think that you're going through "the terrible twos" a little late, but this is a normal part of early life for young children. To me you are a very sweet little boy, and your grandma Susan felt the same way. Most of the time when I'm with you, you are very respectful and you listen to your mommy and daddy. I love it when you politely say 'thank you' so often.

I especially love it when you call me 'granpabob', like its one word. I find it funny (but I don't laugh out loud when it occurs) when you stomp your foot, make a fist, and say "knock it off." I wonder who you learned that from? When you visited my house recently with your family, it was very funny to see Logan do and say exactly the same thing.

It is so much fun for me watching you play with your Thomas the Train toys, especially hearing you tell me the names of every engine, and listening to the train noises you make as you guide your trains around the floor, and on the tracks you put together. Maybe someday you will get to ride on a real train.

Little brothers look up to their older brothers and they want to do the same things that the older boy does. When you're a little older, you will be very helpful to Logan, and to mommy and daddy, by helping Logan to learn good behaviors. The best way to teach is by example—Logan watches everything that you do, just as you watch everything that Sadie and your parents do. Learning to set a good example is an important part of growing up to be a man that God, and your parents, and friends, will be proud of. I'm already very proud of you.

Love,
Grandpa Bob

Dear Logan,

Our fifth grandchild, soon to be two years old. I haven't known you very long, yet I love you as dearly as my other four grandchildren. When you came to visit me recently you were walking and running. It was the first time I'd seen you walking and it was wonderful to watch you get around so well. You had grown so much since the last time I was with you. It touched my heart deeply that even though you'd not seen me in quite a long while, as soon as you arrived you were not hesitant to come to me and let me hug and hold you. It was a special show for grandpa Bob to watch you with Dillon and Sadie as you interacted with each other. You resemble Sadie more than Dillon with your light-colored hair and sharp features. You're young enough that things like hair color could change a lot as you grow older. When I was your age my hair was very blonde. Eventually it turned brown. Now it's mostly gray ... whatever hair I have left.

I will continue to enjoy watching you grow in the years to come and hope to see you more often.

Love,
Grandpa Bob

<<<<<< >>>>>>

I pray that I may be around long enough to continue to watch my five grandchildren grow and prosper. You are all such beautiful blessings from God, for which I am so thankful. You are very fortunate to have moms and dads who love you deeply and who will always try their best to provide you with the example, skills, and motivation, to live your lives in ways that please God.

With much love for each of you,
Grandpa Bob

Epilogue

I wrote this collection of memories during the journey along my path of grieving the loss of my wife, Susan. I don't yet know when I'll reach the end of this path. I sense that it will be a long journey.

I've concluded that this journal of memories both sweet and bitter is part of the journey I'm on. Writing about it helped to fuel my soul and spirit so that when I awoke to face each new day, I did so looking forward to emptying some of my pent up sadness and despair onto these pages. Grief was purged, or at least lessened to some degree, each time I set down a memory of the life that Susan and I shared for so many wonderful years.

The days of uncontrolled, gut-wrenching sorrow are tapering off very slowly. There was a time when I wondered if and when this would happen, would it be evidence that I hadn't grieved long enough or hard enough? I no longer feel this way now that the intensity has waned. The scarring of grief is so much more than I could have imagined. I am now convinced that this writing adventure is what needed to happen to help me recover. I cannot imagine anyone continuing to grieve as though every day was the first day of loss, and not suffer serious emotional and physical problems.

The size of the hole in my heart will never be smaller. But it is being slowly refilled, refilled with something different from what was there before. I cannot explain what the new substance consists of, but I know it is happening because I can feel it. Call it the result of a spiritual MRI, for want of a better way to explain what I'm feeling. And this slow refilling of my wound gradually is taking the pain level down one slow notch at a time.

The statistics found in mortality tables show that in the first six months following the loss of a spouse, the surviving spouse's mortality increases by more than 50%. This means that in the first six months, surviving spouses die at a rate that is 50% higher than those who did not suffer the loss of a spouse. I worried about this off and on through the first six months, and as the weeks and months drifted by, I could understand why this was true. Heartache, depression, anxiety, loss of appetite, isolation, sleeplessness, confusion: These things can be virtual killers during a time of great weakness and vulnerability.

I believe now that I can and will survive and be a relatively healthy widower. This is the first time I've used this word, 'widower'. It is a strange word that I suppose I'll need to get used to. I may die in moments, or many years down the road, but I'm pretty confident that when this happens it won't be caused solely by grief for my sweet Susan.

I commented briefly about belief systems in the introduction to this book. To satisfy presumed curiosity that some readers may have, here, in a nutshell is my belief system.

I believe that Jesus of Nazareth, the Jewish carpenter, was and is the Son of God, sent to Earth in a uniquely miraculous manner, to become the Ultimate sinless sacrifice for the fallen human race, paying a debt He did not owe, for our imperfections. To those who accept Him as mankind's Messiah, whom the Bible, both the Old and the New Testaments describe as such with rather stark clarity, He is the doorway to eternal life with Him in His Heavenly kingdom.

Susan now dwells in this Heavenly abode, and I know that we will see each other again, there in that place, when I am called home. This unshakeable conviction, above all else, prevented my grief from literally killing me.

I hope that these very personal windows that I've opened into my life and Susan's life have given you some enjoyment, and insight on love, relationships, faith, marriage, parenting, and grief, that will serve to be of some benefit to you in your own life journey.

Finally, if there is someone that you love, whom you haven't told recently that you love them, especially if it's your spouse, *say it to them now!*

Acknowledgments

These writings were not initially intended to be a book; they kind of morphed into one. It is certainly not a complete biography of either my sweet Susan or myself; its more a select collection of memories that span our relationship over half a century, brought to fruition as the result of my loss.

I found great comfort in writing about my life with Susan, and much to my surprise, my writings became extensive as memories begot memories. I received encouragement to continue to write from a number of dear people in my life with whom I shared bits and pieces of my writings, some of whom suggested that I consider pulling it all together as a book.

Foremost I acknowledge and thank my Lord, Jesus Christ, who changed the world, and changed my life. Because I believe in who He was and is, I tightly hold on to the promise of an everlasting life for the human spirit after death, in a Heaven within which there is everlasting peace and joy for its inhabitants. This belief has been a strong lifeline through my maelstrom of grief, knowing that Susan is now eternally with God in His perfect Heaven, fully healed, and rejoicing, and that we will see each other again someday, in that place.

My children have been a great support to me, especially my son, Adam, who, because of his living a couple of hours away, his strength of character, and his love, helped me through the most difficult and bewildering early days after my loss, and his loss too, and still is so helpful to me today. Though it may seem like a small thing, the regular phone calls from all my children are a great blessing and comfort for me.

Many friends encouraged me to write about my memories and to share them with others. I'm sure that I cannot remember all of them; you know who you are. I thank you with all my heart for your love and friendship through the most difficult time of my life.

Last, but far from least, I owe an enormous debt of gratitude to my dear friend and editor, Dr. Randall VanderMey, Chair, Department of English, Westmont College, an accomplished author and teacher. Without his willingness to suffer through my amateur hodge-podge of writings, offering his candid and invaluable edits and reflections, this book would undoubtedly be a lesser product.

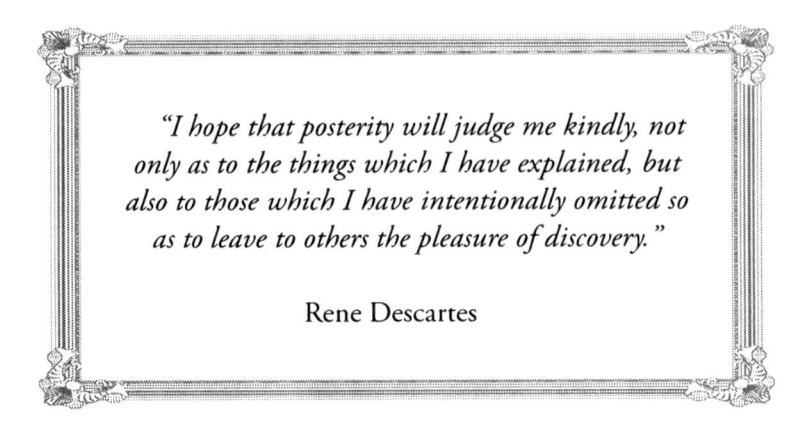

> *"I hope that posterity will judge me kindly, not only as to the things which I have explained, but also to those which I have intentionally omitted so as to leave to others the pleasure of discovery."*
>
> Rene Descartes